PUFFIN BOOKS

UNEARTHED: AN ENVIRONMENTAL HISTORY OF INDEPENDENT INDIA

Meghaa Gupta's tryst with environmentalism began in 2013, when she was commissioned to compile a book on environmental courses and careers for students in India. From passionate teachers and students to eminent professionals, the journey exposed her to the fascinating work being done in this field. Her writing has also appeared in *TerraGreen*, *Careers360* and *The Hindu* and she has contributed to WWF-India's One Planet Academy. She is deeply interested in exploring how young people relate to the natural world and has conducted a series of workshops with school and college students in association with WWF-India. Meghaa works in children's publishing and this is her third book.

ADVANCE PRAISE FOR THE BOOK

'This is a carefully researched and lucidly written environmental history of India since Independence. The book covers a wide range of themes— water, forests, agriculture, air and water pollution—with balance and clarity. The illustrations and character portraits add immensely to the book. While it is specifically oriented towards schoolchildren, I recommend *Unearthed* to Indians of all ages seeking an accessible overview of our environmental challenges'—Ramachandra Guha, author of *Environmentalism: A Global History*

'*Unearthed* gives you all the important information about revolutions, movements, sectors and technology that emerged in India after Independence and their effects on the environment. I would personally recommend this book because it is told in the form of a story, has comics and is very interesting to read. The book is good for anyone who wants to know about the environment or climate change'—Ridhima Pandey, young climate activist and speaker at 2019 UN Climate Action Summit

UNEARTHED
AN ENVIRONMENTAL
HISTORY OF
INDEPENDENT
INDIA

MEGHAA GUPTA

ILLUSTRATIONS BY ADITI SHASTRY

PUFFIN BOOKS
An imprint of Penguin Random House

PUFFIN BOOKS

USA | Canada | UK | Ireland | Australia
New Zealand | India | South Africa | China

Puffin Books is part of the Penguin Random House group of companies
whose addresses can be found at global.penguinrandomhouse.com

Published by Penguin Random House India Pvt. Ltd
4th Floor, Capital Tower 1, MG Road,
Gurugram 122 002, Haryana, India

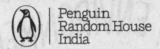

Penguin
Random House
India

First published in Puffin Books by Penguin Random House India 2020

Text Copyright © Meghaa Gupta Aggarwal 2020
Illustration copyright © Aditi Shastry 2020

ISBN 9780143450917

Book design and layout by Aditi Shastry
Typeset in Charter by Manipal Technologies Limited, Manipal

Printed at Repro India Limited

www.penguin.co.in

MIX
Paper from
responsible sources
FSC® C047271

To my motherland and my mother

Contents

Contents

Foreword

Unearthed: An Environmental History of Independent India is a book for our times. A book written for the young of today and the young of tomorrow.

The world has changed. The biosphere has sent us repeated warnings, but we chose to ignore them. While some insist that now is all that matters, empirical data confirms that without learning from the past we will never be able to negotiate a path through the minefield we have laid between now and the future.

What were the hopes and aspirations of our founding fathers and mothers? How far have we veered from Gandhiji's dream for India? Are children at the centre of our ambitions of development? Is the quality of life of the vast majority of Indians going up . . . or down? Is India a safer place today than it was thirty, twenty or even ten years ago? Is rural India being colonized by urban India? Are our economists and bankers interested in the health of our people, or the profit margins on their balance sheet?

For many years, very powerful people (mainly politicians, bureaucrats and businessmen) who should have known better, claimed that India is 'too poor' a country to worry about 'westernized' notions of environmental concerns such as climate change, rising sea levels, deforestation and pollution. How misguided such people were! How badly they have damaged our country! How persistently they continue to harm us!

What would India be like in twenty or thirty years, if each parliamentarian were to keep children at the centre of his or her development barometer? Suppose by some miracle we were able to convince MLAs and MPs to spend the rest of their terms looking after their constituencies by cleaning up rivers, lakes and wells, and by reducing air pollution as ways of implementing preventive health measures . . . Surely our country would be no worse than it is today. By contrast, if the current economic agenda is implemented without let or hindrance for much longer, I believe life will become unliveable for most.

Unearthed: An Environmental History of Independent India by Meghaa Gupta should be essential reading not only for children but also our political and corporate leaders. Understanding the history of this country post-Independence is vital. We cannot blame our current environmental crisis on our colonial past alone. An acknowledgement and deeper understanding of where we have gone wrong will hopefully help us forge a new chapter in our country's environmental path—one in which we opt for small and micro-hydel schemes instead of large dams, one that relies on sustainable land-use practices to improve agriculture, one that appreciates the immense biodiversity values of our wildernesses, one that chooses to develop 'nature capital' rather than exhaust it.

Children are the most powerful agents of positive, environmental change. They not only have the legitimacy, but the fire to actually take the small and large actions vital to the task of reversing the ecological rot that adults have in mind for the planet. As Meghaa writes in the introduction, at its heart, this book is 'about how our choices and actions have impacted our environment.' Let us show our children that while in the past, our chosen heroes had to fight nature, subdue nature, force it to bend to our will . . . tomorrow's heroes will be the ones that resurrect our wounded Eden. Individuals that remind us of the virtues of respect and humility when dealing with forces of nature, which are far more powerful and efficient than any human invention.

Bittu Sahgal
Editor, Sanctuary Asia

Introduction

If you were a child growing up in 1947, your life would have been shockingly different from what it is today. The city you live in today might have been a village; you may have lived without electricity, relying on *pankhas* to keep yourself cool and kerosene lamps for lighting. You wouldn't have known about electronic gadgets, such as televisions, computers and mobile phones, which surround us today. You may have had to walk several kilometres to go to school and probably not have sat in a car. You also wouldn't have heard of pollution or climate change.

The story of how independent India went from being a largely underdeveloped, rural land to one of the fastest growing countries in the world is a fascinating account of development. Development gave us many comforts that we often take for granted today. But it came at a price—the takeover of nature.

Large dams were built on free-flowing rivers to supply water for irrigation and drinking, and hydroelectricity for industries. Large-scale deforestation that had been perpetuated by the British was continued, to source raw materials for Indian industries and clear land for agriculture and the growing human population. Forests were also drowned by dams. Wildlife was threatened by a shrinking habitat and the danger of poaching.

So, was development wrong? After all, even though it made our lives easier, it also damaged the environment.

Development isn't a problem, but thoughtlessly damaging the environment certainly is. For example, if we chop down a forest to build a thermal power plant that produces electricity and employs people, it benefits people who need employment and electricity. But it also destroys the homes of many wild animals and without trees, sources of life-giving oxygen are greatly reduced. If the power plant then goes on to pollute the air with smoke (and keep in mind, there are no trees to absorb the pollutants), the polluted air will make people sick and they will not be able to work. So the power plant too won't be able to function well.

However, what if the power plant is built in a way that doesn't destroy an entire forest and doesn't emit large amounts of pollutants? What if lots of trees are planted to make up for the ones that have been chopped down?

Unearthed: An Environmental History of Independent India is, at its heart, a story about how our choices and actions have impacted our environment. It isn't always happy, but neither is it always sad. For example, free India was keen to industrialize. But in 1984, our industrial development was jolted when deadly gas leaked out of a factory in Bhopal and thousands of people died within a few days. We had suffered the worst industrial disaster in the world. But in its wake, we passed a landmark law to protect our environment. We started questioning unsafe industrialization and many years later, we became one of the few countries in the world with a special court just for taking up cases related to environmental justice.

The year 2020 will go down in history as the year of the coronavirus pandemic—an infectious respiratory disease that has claimed scores of lives around the world. To stop the spread of the disease, India asked its people to cease all social activities and stay locked in their homes. Technology, such as computers, phones and the internet, has helped a lot of people work from home, study online and remain in touch with friends and family members.

With humans staying in, wildlife has ventured out. Birds twitter in the silence. Deer and antelopes have been spotted strutting on the streets. Dolphins have been seen swimming in clean waters. Pollution levels have dropped drastically because industrial activity has been reduced and very few vehicles are allowed on the roads.

However, the economy that drives all development is nearly collapsing. Industries that manufacture many products that we use have shut down. People who work in these industries have lost their jobs. Labourers who came from villages and towns to work in these industries near the cities have been hit especially hard. Since means of transport have been limited, they've been walking hundreds of kilometres to return to their towns and villages.

Our prehistoric ancestors may have survived on nature alone, but we need both—nature as well as development. Emphasizing on one while neglecting the other will harm everyone in the long run. Perhaps, having witnessed the resurgence of wildlife and pollution-free days in the wake of this pandemic, we will all be inspired to maintain the golden balance between the two.

Today, we study about the environment in school. From pollution to climate change, environmental problems are affecting our lives in ways beyond our imagination. What you're about to read now reflects upon the history behind these problems in the hope that knowing our past will help us all shape a better future.

And who better than children—inheritors of our land and guardians of the future.

Meghaa Gupta
15 April 2020

1

When You Divide a Land

It was a terribly hot July in 1947 when a British lawyer named Cyril Radcliffe first arrived in India. The country was tense. Communal riots had broken out between Hindus, Sikhs and Muslims. It had been announced that British India would be partitioned to create Pakistan, a separate country for Muslims. Radcliffe had been saddled with the dreadful job of dividing the land in a way that would leave a majority of Hindus and Sikhs in India and Muslims in Pakistan. So far, he had had nothing to do with India and somehow this had qualified him as the best person for this job—he would not be partial.

The clock was ticking and he had a little over a month to complete the job. So he locked himself in a room and started drawing borders on outdated maps as quickly as possible. These borders, which came to be called the Radcliffe Lines, split the British-era provinces of Punjab and Bengal almost in half to form India, West Pakistan (now simply Pakistan) and East Pakistan (now Bangladesh).

Once Radcliffe finished, he left India immediately and never came back.

Chaos Everywhere

When Radcliffe's borders were made public a day after Independence, there was chaos everywhere. The villages were in one country and their fields were in the other. In some cases, the front doors of houses opened in India, while their back doors opened in Pakistan. Lakhs of people discovered that they were not in a country they expected to be included in, so they began to flee from one to the other. By and large, Muslims fled from India that had a majority of Hindus, while Hindus and Sikhs fled from Pakistan that had a majority of Muslims.

There was so much suspicion, anger and fear between the communities that more than 10 lakh people died in the bloodbath that followed Partition.

Make a Trip

In the city of Amritsar, Punjab, close to the famous Golden Temple, is the world's first Partition Museum. It was opened on the 70th anniversary of the Partition.

Even though hundreds of refugee camps were created for people fleeing from one country to another, they were simply not enough. Perhaps no one had anticipated that close to 1.5 crore people would be displaced because of Partition.

5,00,000

The approximate number of refugees who arrived in Delhi after Partition

The stories of refugees are often about the trauma caused by Partition. But if you listen carefully, you will also find an environmental point of view.

Lack of Resources

When a large number of people suddenly descend upon a small area and start living there, the available resources fall short, especially food and clean drinking water.

That was the case with most refugee camps. People were often given only a limited helping of dal and rice or a single chapati per person. The situation was so desperate that even when a family lost a member, they continued to claim food in the person's name. Not only was the food too little, it also lacked sufficient nutrition. This led to deficiency diseases such as night blindness and rickets. Children were the worst affected, as their growing bodies needed food and water more than the adults.

Things only got worse because there were hardly any toilets. With human waste and sewage piling up in the open, these camps were extremely filthy. Diseases like cholera, which are caused by consuming food and water contaminated by bacteria found in human waste, were extremely common.

India's epic toilet building spree

Lack of toilets is such a big problem in India that in 2014, it began the greatest toilet-building spree in human history by deciding to construct more than 10 lakh toilets in five years!

Medical care was scarce, even though people were falling sick. The number of dead bodies kept mounting and disposal of corpses became a major problem.

Within a few months of Partition, the season began to change. Winter set in and many people died because they could not save themselves from the cold. These were the 'weather casualties' of Partition.

The refugee crisis created by Partition was among the worst in India's history. But Partition didn't just divide people, it also divided natural resources such as mountains, rivers and forests. One of the most serious problems came from the partitioning of rivers.

Fighting Over Water with Pakistan

The Indus river originates in the Tibetan Plateau near Lake Manasarovar, flows into India and then into Pakistan, before merging with the Arabian Sea.

The partition of Punjab divided the Indus and five of its main tributaries—Jhelum, Chenab, Sutlej, Ravi and Beas. It's because of these five tributaries that Punjab is called 'the land of five rivers'.

Punjab has always been an agricultural state, defined by its endlessly green farms. Both India and Pakistan needed the waters of these rivers for irrigating the farms. Pakistan was especially worried. Not only were all these rivers flowing in from India, but Chenab, Sutlej, Ravi and Beas, unlike Indus and Jhelum, ran for several kilometres in India before entering Pakistan.

After years of disputes over water sharing and temporary agreements, India and Pakistan signed the Indus Waters Treaty in 1960. As per this treaty, the waters of Sutlej, Ravi and Beas belong to India, while Pakistan controls Indus, Jhelum and Chenab. The Indus Waters Treaty is often held up as a model for water sharing agreements. But it has faced difficult times when the two countries have been at loggerheads and India has raised the threat of scrapping it.

Fighting Over Water with Bangladesh

In Bengal, the Radcliffe lines partitioned the Ganga and crossed over fifty-four smaller rivers. However, the Ganga flowed very briefly through East Pakistan before emptying into the Bay of Bengal. So East Pakistan had virtually no control over its waters and they could be diverted easily by India.

In 1951, India decided to construct the Farakka barrage, a type of dam, a little over 16 kilometres from the border with East Pakistan. The barrage would divert large amounts of Ganga water to the Hooghly river flowing along the port city of Kolkata (then Calcutta). Protests broke out in East Pakistan where a majority of people survived on agriculture and needed the river water for irrigation. Work on the barrage had to be stopped because of the protests. However, twenty years later, in 1971, East Pakistan fought a war against West Pakistan and gained independence to become Bangladesh.

India had helped East Pakistan in the war and, in gratitude, Bangladesh allowed the construction of the Farakka barrage. In 1975, Ganga water was finally diverted.

Predictably, this led to many problems in Bangladesh. Agriculture was hard hit, as was fishery, the second most important means of subsistence in the country. It also reduced the supply of fresh river water in the fragile mangrove forests of the Sundarbans in Bangladesh and harmed the ecosystem.

In December 1996, the two countries signed a 30-year water-sharing treaty. The treaty depends heavily on the volume of water flowing in the Ganga at the Farakka barrage and does not fix a specific amount of water to be released to Bangladesh. This has created a problem for Bangladesh, especially in years when rainfall is poor and the volume of water at the barrage has fallen drastically. That's why many people in Bangladesh consider this a failed treaty and tensions continue between the two countries.

The Long Road Ahead

Partition was a rocky start for newly independent India and a lasting legacy of its colonial past. But India continued to march ahead. It not only wanted to transform agriculture and uplift its farmers, but also wanted to industrialize. Large dams built over its numerous large rivers occupied a special place in these plans. They would not only provide irrigation for agriculture but also electricity to run industries. Thus, began the country's conquest of nature.

2

'Green' Revolution?

One of the biggest problems facing newly independent India was hunger—it had a little over 30 crore people and not enough food for all.

The food that reaches us depends on how much farmers are able to grow, harvest and supply in markets. Sometimes crop yields are affected by bad climatic conditions, diseases that infect the crops or pests such as rats and locusts. Humans can also affect food supply. For example, dishonest middlemen may hoard large quantities of food they buy from farmers instead of sending it to markets. Soon enough, there is a severe shortage and they sell the food at such high prices that most people cannot afford it. Sometimes, farmers themselves end up growing more non-food crops such as cotton. All these factors can lead to food shortage.

When food shortage becomes serious, spreads over a large area and affects a large number of people, it's called a famine. Just a few years before Independence, India suffered one of its worst famines—the Bengal famine of 1943 that killed nearly 30 lakh people.

Buying Food

Independent India was determined to uplift its farmers and feed all its people so it never had to face a famine again. That's why agriculture became our greatest priority in the years after Independence and land under cultivation was considerably increased. However, agriculture was underdeveloped and relied heavily on rainfall. When the rains arrived on time, agricultural produce increased, but when they didn't, we suffered. To make up for food shortage, India began to buy tonnes of food grains, mainly wheat, from other countries. They arrived at our shores in ships, before being distributed to people across the country. That's why we were said to be living a 'ship-to-mouth' existence.

But buying food wasn't easy. Independent India didn't have a lot of money and buying so much food was making us poorer by the day. Besides, being dependent on other countries for something as basic as food is never a good idea. What if they suddenly stopped supplies? In fact, in the mid-1960s, the US did curb its wheat supply to India.

To make up for food shortage, the government tried all sorts of measures, including rationing. Under this system, people could only buy a limited amount of food grains for consumption. Yet, nothing seemed to work. By the 1960s, India's population had crossed 45 crore and back-to-back droughts meant the threat of another famine loomed large.

The drive to save food and prevent wastage was so strong that Lal Bahadur Shastri, the second Prime Minister of India urged people to fast, once every week.

Origins of the Green Revolution

In 1944, when India was still fighting for Independence, more than 15,000 kilometres away a green revolution was quietly brewing at the International Maize and Wheat Improvement Centre in Mexico. Scientists, led by Norman Borlaug, were trying to increase the production of food crops—especially rice and wheat—in the country. The results were astounding. By 1964, Mexico, which had been importing half its wheat, was producing enough to export five lakh tonnes.

NORMAN BORLAUG

Norman Borlaug was awarded the Nobel Prize in 1970 for his game-changing contribution to the Green Revolution. He is often called the Father of the Green Revolution.

What was the secret behind this remarkable success? The institute in Mexico had developed a variety of dwarf wheat that was far superior to ordinary wheat. Not only was it resistant to several diseases and pests but it also produced two to three times more grain. That's why these crops were called High-Yielding Varieties and their seeds were called 'miracle seeds'.

These miracle seeds came with a whole new way of farming. They needed chemical fertilizers to provide nutrition, pesticides to destroy pests, ample water supply through irrigation and use of advanced farm equipment for activities like tilling the land, sowing seeds and harvesting.

Green Revolution in India

In 1965, the Green Revolution was introduced in Punjab, Haryana and western Uttar Pradesh. Demonstrations were held in fields, promotions were made through national media such as All India Radio and trained farmers were encouraged to teach others. The farmers were spellbound by the miraculous yields and took to the revolution enthusiastically. That's how the Green Revolution, which began as a small government programme called the High Yielding Varieties Programme, became a mass movement led by farmers.

Within a few years, India was growing enough food grains to not only feed itself but also to export to other countries. But it also began to realize the problems of the Green Revolution.

BEFORE AND AFTER
THE GREEN REVOLUTION

Bullock cart

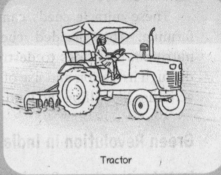

Tractor

Organic manure

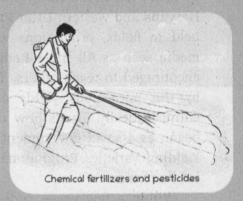

Chemical fertilizers and pesticides

Praying for rain

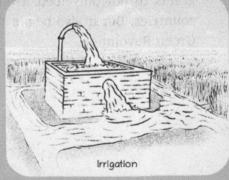

Irrigation

When 18-year-old Mankombu Sambasivan Swaminathan witnessed the horrors of the 1943 Bengal famine, it changed his life. He came from a family of doctors and had even gotten a seat in a medical school. But after witnessing the famine, he decided to help his country fight hunger. Swaminathan became an agricultural scientist and went on to play an important role in introducing and implementing the Green Revolution in India. That's why he is often called the Father of the Green Revolution in India.

DR M. S. SWAMINATHAN

Cost of Production

Before the Green Revolution, farmers would grow local varieties of crops that were best suited to the soil and climate in the area. Seeds were saved during each harvest and sown again. They were cultivated using old-fashioned wooden ploughs, waterwheels, bullock carts and organic manure, and usually irrigated by the rain. However, the High Yielding Varieties of the Green Revolution were not suited to this age-old way of farming.

Farmers had to buy their seeds as well as special chemical fertilizers and pesticides to grow them. They also had to spend on advanced equipment to farm and supply water on time. Many farmers couldn't afford all this without borrowing money. Many of them also failed to fully understand the new ways. Over the years, yields began to decline and the success of the Green Revolution was largely confined to Punjab, where farmers were relatively wealthier and better educated about the new ways. In some places, farmers also started returning to growing local varieties of crops using the old ways of farming (*see page 74*).

Chemical Overdose

Farmers who weren't used to the new ways often used more chemical fertilizers and pesticides than needed. As these chemicals seeped into the soil, they destroyed its natural fertility. So farmers had to use a larger quantity of chemical fertilizers to keep their soil fertile. In 1950–51, farmers were using about 69,000 tonnes of mostly organic fertilizer. But by 2006, they were using more than 1,90,00,000 tonnes of mostly chemical fertilizers. Over time, the soil simply stopped responding to the chemicals and many swathes of land became infertile.

The chemicals also seeped into the groundwater and polluted the water bodies nearby. Some of these chemicals turned to vapour once they were sprayed and polluted the air. Water and air pollution poisoned plants and animals and also caused serious health problems for people.

One Crop, Many Problems

Different crops have different needs. For example, some need more water and different nutrients than others. Before the Green Revolution, farmers were planting more than one type of crop in their fields. If they planted rice one season, they would plant pulses the next. This is known as crop rotation.

Crop rotation allows the soil to recharge nutrients that a certain crop does not need. Also, between harvesting one crop and sowing the next, farmers leave the soil unploughed for a while—literally giving it a break.

The Green Revolution was especially favourable to wheat and rice. That's why more and more farmers began to grow just these crops. Growing just one type of crop is known as monocropping.

Large areas of land were cleared of vegetation—mainly trees—to make way for monocropping. Without trees, there was nothing to absorb extra water from irrigation or rainfall, or to hold the soil and prevent it from being eroded by wind or water. Monocropping not only worsened the soil, it also reduced the variety of crops grown in India.

According to the Food and Agriculture Organization (FAO), because of monocropping, more than 60% of agriculture around the world is dominated by just nine types of plants— sugar cane, maize, rice, wheat, soybeans, potatoes, oil palm fruit, sugar beet and cassava.

So, Was the Green Revolution Successful?

There are many people who criticize the Green Revolution today. They say it impoverished farmers and damaged our natural environment with chemicals and monocropping. It's hard to overlook these problems. But food shortage was so acute by the 1960s that without the Green Revolution, India would have suffered a massive famine. In 1968, American biologist Paul Ehrlich wrote *The Population Bomb*—a globally renowned book in which he boldly claimed that the battle to feed all of humanity was over because in a few years, countless people would starve to death! According to him, it was impossible for India to be able to feed itself by 1971.

The Green Revolution squashed Ehrlich's claims. Yet, crores of poor people, especially children, continue to remain hungry. They either don't get enough to eat, or the food they eat isn't nutritious enough. Due to these problems, many children are either too short for their age or weigh too little or both. They're so weak that many of them die before they are five years old. The biggest worry for poor people around the world is where they'll get their next meal from. That's food insecurity.

The Green Revolution taught us many lessons about the triumphs and failures of modern agriculture. Today, it's estimated that by 2050, India's population will cross 160 crores. What we need is to ensure better storage, transportation and distribution of food grains and to find more sustainable forms of modern agriculture to fight growing food insecurity.

3
Dammed!

It's no coincidence that human civilizations around the world came up along riverbanks. Being near a river gave humans a ready source of water for drinking and fishing. The land along rivers is usually fertile so they were able to grow food and water their crops. Rivers also allowed them to travel on boats.

But to make the best use of river water, they needed to control it. Imagine if they had to go to a river and fill buckets of water for drinking, watering crops or using at home . . . they would have spent all their time filling buckets. That's why they began to build dams that controlled the flow of rivers and brought water to them.

A dam is like a wall built across a river. It stops the river from flowing forward and collects its water in one place, also called a reservoir. Water from the reservoir is what comes to our homes, schools, farms and industries through a network of canals and pipes connected to the dam. Once enough water has been collected to meet the needs of an area, the rest is released and the river continues flowing.

A King and an Engineer

The Chola king, Karikala was greatly troubled by the river Kaveri which ran through his kingdom, in present day Tamil Nadu. It would frequently change its course and flood the surrounding areas with large amounts of sediment, making them uncultivable for long periods of time. To control the river, Karikala built the Kallanai Dam across it, more than 2000 years ago. It was more than 1000 feet long and between 40 to 60 feet wide, and it helped to irrigate thousands of acres of land.

Karikala built such a good dam that hundreds of years later, the British engineer Arthur Thomas Cotton used its design for building other irrigation works on the Kaveri and Godavari rivers in Tamil Nadu and Andhra Pradesh. These projects were so successful in irrigating the land and boosting agriculture that Cotton became hugely popular among the people of these states. Many compared him to the legendary king Bhagiratha, who was said to have brought the river Ganga from the heavens on to Earth. In fact, you can find close to 3000 statues of the man in districts surrounding the river Godavari in Andhra Pradesh!

Make a Trip

If you ever happen to make a trip to Rajahmundry in Andhra Pradesh, do visit the Sir Arthur Cotton Museum there. Located near the Dowleswaram Barrage built by him, it has nearly 100 photographs and 15 machine tools used for the construction of the barrage.

Dam-building Spree

When India became Independent in 1947, it had a basic military and administration, but it hardly had any industries. Most of its population survived on agriculture. But agriculture was extremely underdeveloped and depended too much on rainfall for irrigation. Food shortages, which eventually led to the Green Revolution (*see page 8*), made things worse. It became urgent for India to modernize and large dams played a very important role in this modernization. They not only provided water for irrigation, they also prevented flooding and generated hydroelectricity (*see page 157*). Since the dams had so many uses, they were called multipurpose dams. Such dams were hugely popular in North America and Russia and now, even India would have them.

The Bhakra Dam on the river Sutlej was the first major project completed in independent India. It was built entirely by Indians, but its chief engineer, Harvey Slocum, was an American. Slocum was a strict disciplinarian. He would come to work sharp at 8 a.m. every day and remain there until late in the evening. He expected the same from everyone working on the project. Once, when the telephone lines broke down, an irritated Slocum wrote to Prime Minister Jawaharlal Nehru that only God could build the Bhakra Dam on time!

5334

Approximate number of large dams in India in the year 2019. Many of them were built between 1970 and 1990.

In July 1954, the Prime Minister visited the dam to launch the project. As he switched on the power station of the dam, aircraft from the Indian Air Force dipped their wings overhead. When he opened the gates of the dam, water from its reservoir rushed out. Seeing the river racing towards them, excited villagers set off home-made firecrackers. In 1963, when the dam was finally functional, a proud Prime Minister dedicated it to the nation, calling it 'the new temple . . . of India'.

Make a Trip

Reservoirs of many dams are also popular tourist spots. The Gobind Sagar Reservoir of the Bhakra Dam is popular for sports such as water skiing, kayaking, water scooter racing and sailing.

Large dams are marvels of modern engineering and the new nation took pride in them. So during the first few decades after Independence, it went on a dam-building spree. However, with large dams came large problems. During the 1970s and the 1980s, two significant movements broke out in India that shed light on the downside of dams.

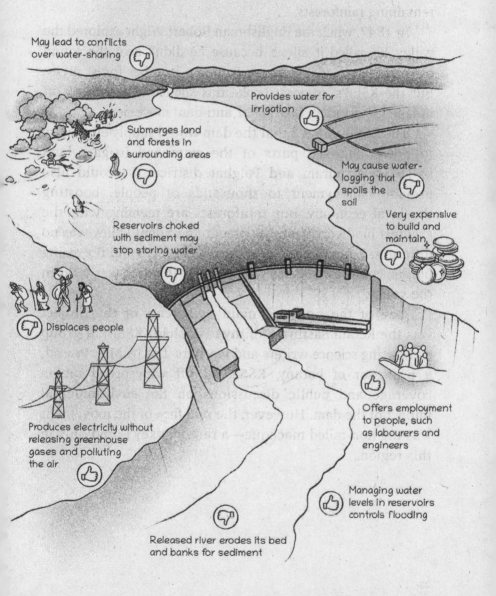

THE PROS 👍 & CONS 👎 OF BUILDING DAMS

May lead to conflicts over water-sharing 👎

Provides water for irrigation 👍

Submerges land and forests in surrounding areas 👎

May cause water-logging that spoils the soil 👎

Very expensive to build and maintain 👎

Reservoirs choked with sediment may stop storing water 👎

Displaces people 👎

Produces electricity without releasing greenhouse gases and polluting the air 👍

Offers employment to people, such as labourers and engineers 👍

Managing water levels in reservoirs controls flooding 👍

Released river erodes its bed and banks for sediment 👎

Save Silent Valley

In 1970, the Kerala State Electricity Board (KSEB) announced a proposal to build a dam across the river Kunthipuzha that flows through the Silent Valley—home to one of India's last remaining rainforests.

In 1847, when the Englishman Robert Wight explored the valley, he called it 'silent' because he didn't hear the sound of the noisy cicadas that are common in other forest areas. But the KSEB's proposal broke this silence and sparked off independent India's first major anti-dam movement.

The KSEB claimed that the dam would supply electricity to power-deprived parts of the state and irrigate land in the Mallapuram and Palghat districts. It would also provide employment to thousands of people, boosting the local economy. But rainforests are teeming with the greatest biodiversity on the planet and Silent Valley was no different. From birds and butterflies to ferns and flowering plants, countless species would suffer if a dam was built in the valley.

One of the first and main opponents of the project was the Kerala Sasthra Sahithya Parishad (KSSP), a group comprising science writers and teachers. Led by M.K. Prasad, a professor of botany, KSSP set off widespread media coverage and public discussions on the environmental impact of the dam. However, the real face of the movement was the lion-tailed macaque—a rare monkey found only in this region.

The lion-tailed macaque is named after its tail that is quite similar to a lion's—can you tell the similarity? It's the tuft of black hair at the end!

Journalist Darryl D'Monte, who passed away in 2019, was among the pioneers of environmental journalism in India. He played an important role in publicizing the Silent Valley movement in national dailies like the *Times of India* and *Indian Express*. In later years, D'Monte also created a forum for environmental journalists to inspire greater reporting on the subject.

DARRYL D'MONTE

23

Between 1971–72, Steven Green, an American scientist who was studying the primates in the area raised concerns on how the dam would impact the lion-tailed macaque. Soon, other well-known naturalists, such as Romulus Whitaker and Salim Ali joined the fray. Saving biodiversity became a rallying call against the dam. People across the country refused to allow the drowning of a rainforest. By 1977, even the International Union for Conservation of Nature (IUCN) was pressurizing the government to abandon the project.

The IUCN is an international organization that works towards the conservation of biodiversity and sustainable use of natural resources. It was founded in 1948. Among other things, it maintains the world's most comprehensive record of the conservation status of different species. This is called the IUCN Red List. Every time you call an animal 'endangered', 'threatened' or 'extinct', you may actually be referring to its status on this red list. For example, the lion-tailed macaque is 'endangered' on the Red List. To read more about this and search the conservation status of an animal you like, log on to https://www.iucnredlist.org.

The KSSP and other opponents were relentless in their arguments against the dam. They claimed that not only would the dam destroy the forest and its biodiversity, but a majority of the electricity produced would also be exported to the neighbouring states of Karnataka and Tamil Nadu. As for the land being irrigated—they said it could also be watered through other, less expensive means.

Under mounting national and international pressure, the state government tried its best to keep the project alive. It refuted claims and tried to convince the public that only a small portion of the forest would be submerged by the dam and no major harm would be done. Committees were set up to assess the environmental impact of the dam. Their reports didn't support it. Finally, in 1983, the project was called off and in 1985, the area was declared a national park.

Even as the Save Silent Valley campaign drew to an end, trouble was brewing in the Narmada Valley . . .

Narmada Bachao Andolan

The river Narmada rises in the Maikal Hills of Madhya Pradesh and criss-crosses the Vindhya and Satpura Mountains before flowing into the Arabian Sea at the Gulf of Khambhat in Gujarat. This journey of about 1300 kilometres abounds in fascinating myths, legends and history.

The Narmada is a treasure trove of prehistoric fossils. Palaeontologists, who study ancient life and search for such fossils, may tell you about the *Rajasaurus*, among the deadliest Indian dinosaurs, that once roamed this land. In fact, its scientific name is *Rajasaurus narmadensis*, which means 'king lizard of the Narmada'!

Tribal communities that have lived along the river for centuries may narrate one of several legends surrounding it. In one of these stories, the great Lord Shiva meditates long and hard to rid the land of a terrible drought. Little beads of sweat run down his body to become a stream flowing down the hills. Suddenly, this stream becomes an enchanting woman. Shiva is so captivated that he names her Narmada, 'one who pleases', and blesses her, saying she would remain holy and unending. Perhaps that's why Lord Shiva is much revered in these parts. The tribal communities believe he gave them their beloved Narmada.

In 1961 though, the story of the Narmada became the saga of the Narmada Valley Project (NVP). One of independent India's grandest enterprises, it sought to cut up the free-flowing river into 3000 small dams, more than 100 medium-sized dams and thirty large dams. The largest of these would be the Sardar Sarovar Dam in Gujarat, the crown jewel of the NVP.

The dams would take the river water to crores of people spread across Madhya Pradesh, Maharashtra, Gujarat and Rajasthan. They would help with irrigation, flood control and supply electricity and drinking water. But they would also drown large areas along the river—forever changing the land and lives of countless people, mostly tribal communities. The Sardar Sarovar Dam alone would drown the homes of around 2,00,000 people. It would also be an ecological disaster. The Narmada Valley was brimming with flora and fauna. It had several forests, many of which, such as Kanha and Panna, had been turned into tiger reserves. Many species of fish, such as hilsa and mahseer, thrived in the river. The dams would endanger hundreds of species of plants and animals.

From the very beginning, the project was plagued by controversies and delays. Even though the foundation stone was laid in 1961, work on the dam could not begin for close to twenty years because quarrels broke out amongst Madhya Pradesh, Maharashtra and Gujarat over who would get how much water and at what cost. Finally, in 1979, the Narmada

Water Dispute Tribunal—set up to settle the quarrel—divided the water and electricity supply amongst the three states. A few drought-prone areas in Rajasthan too would get water because of the dams. Since the construction of the Sardar Sarovar Dam would displace the largest number of people, Gujarat was to pay for resettlement and rehabilitation.

The tribunal wanted the displaced to at least regain the life they had been living before displacement and it laid out elaborate plans for their resettlement and rehabilitation. As much as possible, they were to be relocated as village units, so they would remain integrated within their communities. The government had to help them with shifting, provide them sources for livelihood and ensure that their basic needs such as housing, transport, fuel, food and drinking water were met. It also had to compensate them for their loss by offering new land and payment for every hectare of land lost.

Facing eviction, some of the settlers began to protest. They didn't want to lose the only life they had known for a long time. Gradually, many people and organizations from outside joined their cause. As more and more people started investigating what was happening in the Narmada Valley, they realized the enormity of the project. It would be next-to-impossible to offer suitable resettlement and rehabilitation to so many people.

Opposition to the dam began to gain momentum and during the 1980s, all those opposing the dam joined hands to form the Narmada Bachao Andolan (NBA) i.e., Save the Narmada Movement. Since the maximum displacement was happening because of the Sardar Sarovar Dam, a large part of their ire was directed at it.

MEDHA PATKAR

Medha Patkar was a young graduate student working towards her PhD in social work when she first arrived in the Narmada Valley. Her father had been a freedom fighter, while her mother worked for women's rights, so she had grown up believing in volunteering and social justice. In 1985, she began researching on resettlement and sharing her findings with the people who were going to be displaced by the Sardar Sarovar Dam. At that time, she was not entirely opposed to the dam. Instead, she was more interested in the successful resettlement and rehabilitation of the people being displaced. But the more she researched, the more she became opposed to the idea of the dam. That's why she became one of the most prominent leaders of the NBA.

Local, national as well as international organizations and celebrities began to associate with the NBA. This wide support base gave it enormous reach and influence.

The NBA organized many campaigns, including marches, rallies, sit-ins and hunger strikes. Even though the government largely refused to engage with it, the NBA received widespread media coverage and managed to exert a lot of pressure on the government.

The NVP was extremely expensive and the government needed to borrow money for it. So it had sought funding from the World Bank. However, the bank was bothered by the resettlement and rehabilitation controversies. The ongoing protests of the NBA and pressure from US-based NGOs supporting the NBA prompted the bank to set up an independent review of the environmental and resettlement impact of the project. The report, released in 1992, was extremely critical of the NVP and raised a number of problems. The World Bank gave India five months to fix the problems raised by the review. When this didn't happen, it cancelled funding.

Stopping the World Bank's funding was among the first and greatest victories of the NBA. International influence also helped the NBA stop many other international organizations from funding the project. By terminating overseas funding, the protesters forced the government to use its own coffers and delayed the project. Soon afterwards, they approached the Supreme Court, asking it to suspend the construction of the dam till the government fulfilled all the resettlement and rehabilitation terms set out by the Narmada Water Dispute Tribunal.

Yet another committee was formed to review the progress of rehabilitation. When this committee found shortcomings, the Supreme Court suspended construction. It was the year 1996, and the NBA had notched up yet another win.

Supporters of the dam realized it was time to wield their power. They began to exert pressure over the court and claimed economic doom if the suspension was not revoked. In 2000, the court took a dramatic U-turn by lifting the suspension even though the resettlement and rehabilitation terms set out by the Narmada Water Dispute Tribunal had not been met.

The NBA's campaigns picked up intensity. Many supporters threatened to drown instead of leaving the land. But work on the dam didn't stop. Instead, supporters of the dam found new ways of challenging the NBA.

In 2017, Prime Minister Narendra Modi inaugurated the Sardar Sarovar Dam—fifty-six years after India's first Prime Minister Jawaharlal Nehru had laid its foundation stone.

Thinking About Damming

Independent India had been extremely enthusiastic in its support of large dams. However, the anti-dam movements in Silent Valley and the Narmada Valley turned the limelight to displacement and the damage to biodiversity caused by large dams. Environmental issues began to feature in the daily news and became a matter of public discussion. They made the nation pause and consider the social and environmental impact of damming its numerous large rivers.

4

India's Milk Revolution

Ghee, ice cream, cheese, paneer, mithai . . . whether you like milk or not, there is no getting away from it in India! In fact, we are among the largest producers and consumers of milk in the world.

But milk lovers didn't always have it so easy. Till the 1970s there was an acute shortage of milk in many parts of India.

Know Your Milk

Milk doesn't just come from cows. People also drink the milk of buffaloes, goats, llamas, reindeer, horses, sheep, camels and yaks. In fact, in India, buffalo milk is more widely consumed than cow milk.

Snaking Queues and Milk Wars

Thirteen-year-old Rajiv would wake up at the crack of dawn—not to go to school, but to line up at a milk depot.

He was the second eldest among his four brothers and was entrusted with this responsibility twice every week. If he reached after 6.30 a.m., the queue would have become much too long—nearly forty- or fifty-people-long! When standing in line got too much to bear, people temporarily left the queue and marked their spot with a stone or a rock. There was no question of asking anyone to save their spot because once the depot window opened, it was a war! You either rushed and got milk or you waited and risked not getting any.

Those were the early 1970s, when in cities like Delhi, getting just two litres of milk for a family of four brothers and their parents was a struggle. The quantity was barely enough, but milk was rationed and that's all that was allowed. Milk powder made up for the deficit. Otherwise, like many others, one would have to rely on crooked vendors who would dilute milk with large quantities of impure water and sell it at astronomical prices.

Milk Crisis in Cities

Even though India had a large population of cattle, what was causing this shortage of milk in cities such as Delhi, Mumbai (formerly Bombay), Kolkata and Chennai (formerly Madras)? The answer was the way most of the milk was supplied to them.

Milk was mainly produced in rural areas and procured by middlemen and contractors, who sold it to suppliers in cities, including depots like the one Rajiv went to. However, this system of procurement was disorganized and couldn't provide enough milk to meet the growing demand.

To make up for the shortage, unscrupulous private vendors in the cities provided milk from their own cattle sheds. Every year, the best, most high-yielding buffaloes were transported to these sheds as soon as they gave birth to a calf. The calves too were brought to help the buffaloes produce milk. The mother was gradually trained to give milk without the presence of her calf. Once mothers were trained, the calves were sent to slaughterhouses, as were the buffaloes that stopped giving milk. Not only was this practice extremely cruel, it was also slowly destroying the best, most high-yielding buffaloes. The unhealthy conditions in these sheds meant the animals were usually stressed and produced poor-quality milk.

But some farmers and an inventive young man in the little town of Anand held an incredible answer to India's milk crisis.

Just like we work best when we're healthy and stress-free, cattle give the best quality milk when healthy and free of stress. Unfortunately, a number of milk producers end up stressing cattle by keeping them in unhealthy conditions, tying them up in congested sheds, not feeding them well and injecting them with harmful chemicals to boost milk production. Having identified these problems, veterinary expert GNS Reddy started Akshayakalpa, an organization that runs dairy farms that value cattle's health. The animals are kept in clean, uncongested sheds. They're given a grass-based diet and their health is closely monitored.

United We Stand

On a fateful Friday, 13 May 1949, Verghese Kurien found himself in the sleepy little town of Anand in Gujarat. The government had sent him to work in its research creamery there. It was the last thing he wanted to do. He was a young engineer with a passion for metallurgy and nuclear physics. In fact, he had also studied these subjects in the US. But the government had funded his foreign education on the condition that he pursued dairy engineering once he returned. If he refused to follow the orders, he would have had to return the grand sum of 30,000 rupees the government had spent on his education. Back in the 1940s, this was a lot of money!

Life in Anand was mighty boring and Kurien found himself looking around for something to do. That's when he bumped into a group of dairy farmers led by Tribhuvandas Patel in Kaira, a district near Anand. They were struggling with the machines in their dairy and needed someone to fix them.

Left to right: Verghese Kurien, Tribhuvandas
Patel and Harichand Dalaya

Milk collected by individual dairy farmers was too little to fetch a good price. So, the farmers had gotten together to form the Kaira District Cooperative Milk Producers Union Limited (KDCMPUL). They pooled in all their milk, so they would have enough to not just sell at a good price, but also to enjoy bargaining power over the buyers.

Kurien was left aghast when he saw the outdated dairy equipment they were using to process their milk. Initially, he helped them repair it but eventually he got them to modernize their operations. In 1950, Kurien left his government job and officially joined the KDCMPUL. He also roped in his friend Harichand Dalaya, a dairying expert, to work for the farmers. After that there was no turning back for this dairying success story that was eventually called AMUL—Anand Milk Union Limited—a name so famous that it would be difficult to find anyone in India who hasn't heard it!

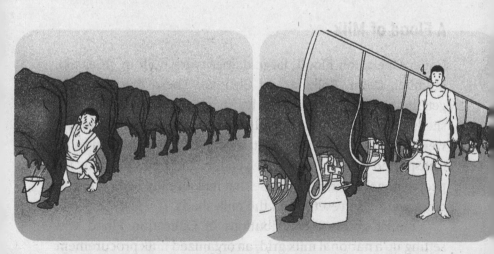

It takes a person an hour to milk six cows by hand. However, with modern milking machines, a person can milk 100 cows in an hour!

Everything about Anand, from its soil and climate to its buffaloes, was average . . . Then how was it that during the 1960s and the 70s, apart from AMUL, almost all other dairies in India had failed and the country was facing a milk crisis? What was the secret behind AMUL's stupendous success? The then prime minister, Lal Bahadur Shastri, needed an answer and he turned to Verghese Kurien.

The answer was very simple. Unlike the other government- and privately-owned dairies, AMUL was owned by dairy farmers. The farmers elected representatives from among themselves to manage the dairy and the representatives hired professionals like Kurien to run it. When AMUL did well, the farmers benefitted the most.

Excited, the prime minister urged Kurien to take this 'Anand model' all over the country. He gave him a free hand to do what was needed. Thus was born India's milk revolution—'Operation Flood'.

A Flood of Milk

Under Operation Flood, large dairies were built in cities like Mumbai, Delhi, Kolkata and Chennai. These dairies would get their milk from cooperative dairying areas, called milk sheds. Hundreds of milk sheds, following the 'Anand model', were set up all over India. Cattle would no longer need to be transported to cities by private vendors and treated cruelly for people to get their milk. Those that had already been taken to cities were also resettled in the milk sheds.

One of greatest contributions of Operation Flood was setting up a national milk grid, an organized milk procurement and delivery system that did away with middlemen, contractors and private vendors. Large quantities of milk from the producers were now directly supplied to hundreds of towns and cities in India through rail and road, as part of the national milk grid.

Operation Flood was a massive success. Started in July 1970, it grew by leaps and bounds. Three decades later, India was one of the largest producers of milk in the world, with numerous dairy cooperatives formed by crores of farmers.

Farmers Turn Movie Producers

In 1976, a movie called *Manthan* was released in India. It spoke about the experiences and emotions of people involved in Operation Flood. Five lakh dairy farmers gave two rupees each to produce the movie that went on to become a blockbuster!

So, What's the Environmental Hang-up?

No one can complain about the importance of Operation Flood, but have you ever wondered about the environmental impact of a large dairy business?

Cows have ruminant stomachs: stomachs with four compartments. They spend six to seven hours a day eating and can chew close to 20 kilograms of food every day! This includes green fodder, such as green grass and legumes, as well as dry fodder, such as hay. Farmers get most dry fodder from crop residues—straws left behind after crops have been harvested. But they struggle with green fodder. Most farmers don't grow green fodder on their fields. Instead, they take their cows for grazing. Overgrazing depletes the green cover near villages.

Currently, India faces a green fodder crisis. However, some villages like Sakwa in Gujarat are solving this problem by stopping overgrazing and conserving soil and water in their green areas. Others, especially in southern states like Andhra Pradesh and Kerala, are cultivating plants like the aquatic fern Azolla that grow easily and quickly and can be used as nutritious green fodder.

Not only do cows eat a lot of food, they also drink several litres of water every day. Nearly 80 to 90% of milk is actually water. The rest of it is proteins, carbohydrates, fat, vitamins and minerals. That's why, to produce one litre of milk, cows need to drink at least three litres of water. High-yielding cows can easily drink more than 150 litres of water every day.

After eating and drinking, cows, just like humans, also belch and fart. These belches and farts release methane, a type of greenhouse gas, into the air. In fact, one dairy cow can emit about 100–150 kilograms of methane every year! Like carbon dioxide, methane also traps heat and contributes to global warming.

So, what does one do? One cannot stop keeping cattle or giving them food and water. Neither can anyone stop them from belching and farting. But dairy producers can always look at other ways to control the environmental impact of this business . . .

Notes for Dairy Producers

Large amounts of water and electricity are used in powering and cleaning dairy farms. Producers can think of reducing water usage and power their plants using renewable energy.

The transportation of milk and milk products over long distances also consumes energy. Luckily, dairy development has ensured that most places get their milk and milk products from milk sheds that are not located too far away. If you want to check where the milk supplied to you is coming from, you can ask the supplier, or check details printed behind the packet.

Today, milk is mostly sold in plastic bottles and pouches that add to our ever-growing garbage problem after they're used. Some milk producers like Mother Dairy are trying to solve this problem by encouraging consumers to turn to token or 'loose milk' from their automated vending machines, which has a lower price and is collected in reusable vessels. By turning to token milk, we can reduce our plastic consumption by 6 grams daily.

So next time, when you're enjoying a milkshake, think of ways in which your love of milk can also become a love of your natural environment.

5
Tiger Tales

Calvin and Hobbes, Winnie the Pooh, The Jungle Book, The Tiger Who Came to Tea, The Hungry Tiger of Oz, Tiger on a Tree . . . Tigers have been popular characters in literature. Unfortunately, outside the pages of books, these majestic cats are becoming rare because they have run into an increasingly invincible enemy . . . humans.

From Turkey to Bali and beyond, there was once a time when nine subspecies of tigers trooped all across Asia. Three of them—the Bali, Javan and Caspian tigers—have vanished forever. The South China tiger is no longer found in its natural habitat. It exists only in captivity. The ones that remain are the Indochinese, Malayan, Sumatran, Amur (Siberian) and our Bengal tigers. In fact, Bengal tigers make up more than half of all the surviving wild tigers in the world.

Hunting Glory

In the 16th century, Mughal emperor Jalal-ud-Din Muhammad Akbar popularized the royal hunt or shikar. It caught on and remained a favourite pastime of the ruling classes for hundreds of years. Unfortunately, the tiger became the ultimate hunting trophy and thousands of tigers were killed by trophy hunters. It might surprise you to know that newly independent India even advertised tiger shikar to lure rich tourists from around the world.

DAILY MIRROR

India

THRILL TO THE
EXCITEMENT OF A
TIGER "SHIKAR"
FOUND ONLY IN THE
JUNGLES OF INDIA.
FISHING & SMALL GAME
HUNTING, TOO, AWAIT THE
ADVENTUROUS SPORTSMAN!
CONTACT TODAY!

GOVT OF INDIA TOURIST OFFICE

Tiger shikar ads appeared in many international dailies in the years before Project Tiger was announced.

Project Tiger

In the early 1970s, India finally woke up to the fact that it was losing its tigers. Large numbers of the big cat had been killed by trophy hunters and just about 1800 remained. Something had to be done fast. So, in 1972 it passed its first environmental law after Independence—the Wildlife Protection Act. Among other things, the act outlawed hunting tigers.

Apart from India, the tiger is also the national animal of Bangladesh, Myanmar, Malaysia, Vietnam and South Korea. Ironically, even though it's the national animal, the tiger has vanished from South Korea.

A year later, in 1973, the tiger toppled the lion, to become India's new national animal and the government launched Project Tiger. Large areas of forest land inhabited by tigers were set aside as reserves protected by the Wildlife Protection Act. Guards patrolled these reserves, protecting them from intruders. People who lived in these areas were relocated. They could no longer use these areas freely. The number of tiger prey, such as deer, antelopes and wild pigs was increased by digging waterholes and sowing cereal crops in forest clearings. Food would no longer be a problem. The tigers thrived. By 1984, we had over 4000 of these big cats. India had successfully created, what remains, the world's most comprehensive tiger conservation initiative.

But there was little time to bask in this glory. Just a few years later, we were in for a second tiger crisis . . .

The Tiger as Medicine and More

Tigers are feared and admired for their strength and boldness. But in many eastern countries, especially neighbouring China, they are also prized for their supposed medicinal value. Traditional Chinese Medicine (TCM) uses almost every part of a tiger to treat a wide variety of illnesses. Tiger bones are especially valuable. They are believed to cure arthritis, rheumatism, back problems, general weakness and headaches. Tiger bones soaked in rice wine are considered a powerful tonic. Tiger parts also make for exotic luxury products.

Horns from rhinos, scales from pangolins, musk glands from musk deer . . . body parts from more than thirty different animal species are used in TCM, threatening their existence.

So great was the demand for TCM and other tiger products that by the 1980s, professional poachers were supplying tiger parts to manufacturers and dealers all the way from India.

Poaching is serious business, often involving international crime syndicates and massive amounts of money. Poachers usually have a vast knowledge about tiger behaviour and distribution. They use this knowledge to target adult tigers, especially males. Adult male tigers are larger, so the poachers get more money for their skin and body parts.

Vanishing Tigers

In 1993, an astonishing 400 kilograms of tiger bones were seized in Delhi. Conservationists warned that poaching was dragging tigers back to the brink of extinction. But nothing was done. In 2004, a scandal broke out at the Sariska Tiger Reserve—it had lost all its tigers. Soon, other tiger reserves like Ranthambore and Panna reported missing tigers. The extent of damage done by poaching was finally in the public eye. Government officials and wildlife wardens who had dismissed earlier warnings could no longer deny these.

The arrest of poachers painted a grim picture. They described how easy it was to kill a tiger. Most reserves were poorly patrolled. Guards who had quit or retired had not been replaced and there were a large number of vacant posts. Most of the remaining guards were much too old. They worked with non-functional equipment and outdated weapons that were no match for the assault rifles used by the poachers. There was nearly no patrolling during the rainy season. Things had been rather easy for the poachers, who often brought in live bait and shot tigers over their kills.

Unfortunately, despite improving the monitoring of tiger reserves, we have not been able to fully control poaching. Even though it has come down, it hasn't disappeared. As long as there is a demand for tiger products, poaching will not stop. After all, people need money and for many, this continues to be a dangerous but well-paying job. In 2009, more than thirty years since the launch of Project Tiger, India had a little over 1700 tigers left. Far fewer than when the project started.

Counting Tigers

One of the other reasons why tiger numbers may have declined is because we've learnt how to count them better! Till the early 2000s, tigers were mainly counted based on their paw prints. While paw prints are unique, the differences are too subtle to tell them apart accurately. That's why this proved to be an unreliable method. Very often, the same tiger was counted multiple times, inflating numbers. Since 2006, the government has been conducting a national census of tigers and other wildlife every four years. This census uses the far more accurate 'camera traps'. Cameras installed in tiger habitats capture photographs that are stored digitally to create a photo database. Every tiger has unique stripes and every time a photograph is clicked, a software compares it against all the others in the database. If the stripes don't match, the camera has clicked yet another tiger and it's added to the database. The cameras also help to guard a reserve and keep an eye out for poachers. Modern science and technology have also given us other tools, such as radio collars fitted on individual tigers to monitor their movement.

2967

Approximate number of tigers in India, according to the 2018 census

The Needs of a Beast

Tigers need large areas to roam and hunt. They're fiercely protective about their territory and will attack any rival that enters it. Sometimes, one reserve isn't enough territory for tigers, so they migrate to others. Reserves created in the early days of Project Tiger were connected to each other through 'corridors' made up of state forests. Tigers used these corridors to migrate. But over the years, these forests have given way to farms, roads, mines and dams. Trees have also been chopped down to meet the growing need for wood and paper. This has stopped tigers from migrating to other forests. With space running out for tigers inside the reserves, many of them have started to venture out into human settlements around the reserves to rest and hunt.

When villagers living in these areas come face-to-face with tigers, it usually creates chaos. They hate the fierce 'cattle-killers' and 'man-eaters'. Under Project Tiger, when a tiger kills a villager, forest officers need to compensate the victim's family and then track and tranquilize the tiger before taking it back into the reserve. This, unfortunately, doesn't solve the problem—the tigers return soon afterwards. However, killing tigers is outlawed. There needs to be sufficient proof of a tiger being a habitual man-eater for the government to allow it to be killed. What do desperate villagers do in such instances? They take the law in their own hands, slaughtering tigers by poisoning, electrocuting, trapping and shooting.

Edward James Corbett, who you might know as Jim Corbett, was one of the first conservationists of British India. Ironically, he was also an exceptional hunter. Corbett enjoyed

EDWARD JAMES CORBETT

stalking man-eating tigers alone on foot. Between 1906 and 1941, he shot twelve to fifteen man-eating tigers, starting with one that had killed more than 400 people. Yet, he believed that it was stress on their habitat that forced tigers to prey on humans and adopt an 'alien' diet.

Saving Tigers

Tigers are apex predators. Where tigers flourish, so do a wide variety of their prey such as deer and wild pig along with hundreds of other animals, plants, insects, birds—all part of the food chain that builds and conserves a forest. So, saving tigers is essentially about saving forests and the wealth of wildlife they sustain.

Tiger Tourism

Crores of rupees are needed to maintain tiger reserves. One of the ways reserves earn money is through tourism. But unregulated tourism, such as an overabundance of hotels and tourist vehicles crowding around a tiger sighting, creates more problems than solutions. It disturbs tigers and their habitat. That's why every tiger reserve needs to have a large area that is almost exclusive to tigers and their prey. This is a 'core' area and the Supreme Court has banned tourism in it.

A large number of people have devoted their lives to tiger conservation. Here are a few. Can you find out about others? Would you like to be like them?

It was at Kanha National Park—the same reserve that served as a setting for Rudyard Kipling's beloved *The Jungle Book*—that **Bittu Sahgal** fell in love with tigers. A few years later, he started India's first environmental news magazine, *Sanctuary Asia*. After that, there was no stopping Sahgal.

BITTU SAHGAL

He launched *Sanctuary Cub*, a bimonthly kid's magazine and went on to produce several wildlife documentaries. In 2000, he founded 'Kids for Tigers', an educational outreach programme to make kids fall in love with tigers and nature— just like he had several decades ago.

When the 23-year-old city boy **Valmik Thapar** entered the Ranthambore National Park, it changed his life forever. He decided to dedicate it to tigers. Today, Thapar is one of the most prolific authors of literature on tigers. He's written more than twenty books about them, apart from a slew of articles in the national press. He's also founded the Ranthambore Foundation that works with people living in the vicinity of the park, to protect wildlife, including the tiger.

VALMIK THAPAR

Belinda Wright's journey with tigers also began at Kanha, where her parents ran a camp for visitors. When she was 20 years old, Belinda joined the National Geographic Society. In the 1980s, she produced the Emmy-award winning documentary, *Land of the Tigers*, filmed in Ranthambore and Kanha. In 1994, Belinda stumbled upon the racket of illegal trade in tiger skins and bones,

BELINDA WRIGHT

when she was secretly offered four tiger skins for sale. She then orchestrated a string of sting operations uncovering smuggling operations. Belinda left film-making and founded the Wildlife Protection Society of India, which has been at the helm of anti-poaching activities, along with several other initiatives. She loved making films, but she loves saving tigers and other wildlife even more.

Ullas Karanth grew up in Puttur, a rural town in the Western Ghats in Karnataka. Surrounded by flora and fauna and encouraged by his parents, he grew up with a love for the wild. This spurred him to become one of the finest conservation zoologists in India. He pioneered the use of camera traps in India and is well-known for his scientific surveys and research on tigers. Much of his work has centred on the Nagarahole National Park in Karnataka. As part of the Wildlife Conservation Society, Dr Karanth was instrumental in introducing a unique course to train wildlife biologists at the National Centre for Biological Sciences in Bengaluru.

ULLAS KARANTH

6

The Price of a Forest

There was a time when large parts of our country were covered in forests. Our ancient ancestors were hunter-gatherers who got everything they needed—food, water, clothing, shelter—from forests. Over time, they learnt how to grow their own food. As they got better at agriculture, they began to replace forests with farms. Centuries went by as farms and grazing farm animals gradually took over forests. Then, in the 18th century, the industrial revolution began . . . history had not yet seen such a mass destruction of forests.

Industrializing the World

The industrial revolution began in Britain. From the clothes people wore to the flour in their kitchens, everything that used to be made by hand, came to be made by machines in factories. People no longer needed to labour for days on end; machines did the work much faster. The industrial revolution also led to the development of railways and ships that transported people and goods such as raw materials and factory-made products from one place to another. All of these

Apart from carbon dioxide, forests absorb a variety of pollutants from air.

One fully grown leafy tree can produce a day's supply of oxygen for up to 4 people!

Water evaporating from the leaves adds moisture to the air and helps to bring rain.

Trees trap water underground and prevent flooding. Slowly, this water gets released into the streams and rivers flowing through the forest.

Roots hold the soil together and stop erosion by wind or water.

Fallen leaves become manure, making the soil more fertile.

Trees with large canopies offer shade and keep our planet cool.

Millions of people live in and around forests, depending directly on them for animal fodder, fuel, wood, leaf manure, traditional medicine and more.

Forests are home to nearly 80% of the plants and animals found on land.

Can you think of other ways in which forests help the environment?

advances depended heavily on raw materials such as wood and coal that usually came from forests.

Throughout its rule, Britain exploited India's forests for its own industrial development. However, things didn't change much even after Independence. India had seen how Britain had progressed because of industrialization and it wanted to do the same. The only difference was that now forest resources began to be exploited by Indian industries to produce everything from thermal power to steel.

Whose Forest Is It, Anyway?

Before British rule, people living within and around forest areas were usually allowed free access to meet their needs for wood and other forest produce. Even though some forest areas were set aside exclusively for royal use, such as hunting preserves, local communities continued gathering plant material and hunting animals not reserved for the royal hunt. However, the British took exclusive control over large forest areas to meet their industrial needs. Access to locals was either banned or severely restricted. Many tribes that survived almost entirely on forests, such as the Phaseparadhis who live in Maharashtra and parts of Madhya Pradesh, were even branded as criminals. This allowed the police to monitor their movements and arrest them easily.

Independent India decriminalized the tribes. But the government continued to control large forest areas. These areas are known as 'reserved' and 'protected' forests. The main difference between 'reserved' and 'protected' forests is that human activities, such as grazing, are completely banned in reserved forests unless permission has been granted, whereas in protected forests these activities are generally allowed unless they've been specifically banned. In 2017, India had close to 600 such areas, mainly comprising wildlife sanctuaries and national parks.

Fighting over forests

Government control over forests made tribal and other forest-dwelling communities 'encroachers' on their own land. Even though the government restricted their rights over forests, industries from outside were allowed to chop down the forests for raw material in many areas. Local people were outraged by the injustice and this led to many conflicts over forest use. One of the most famous examples of such a conflict is the Chipko movement from the 1970s.

The Importance of Hugging Trees

The Chipko movement was born in the Himalayan state of Uttarakhand, which at the time was part of Uttar Pradesh. The state, which borders China, witnessed a period of rapid development after the Indo-China war of 1962. Roads that had been built during the war opened up the state to industries hungry for Himalayan conifers. The government that managed these forests began to allow industries to fell trees for wood and resin.

Not wanting to be left behind, the local people formed cooperatives that competed with the industries to ask for permission to get wood and resin from the forests. The Dashauli Gram Swarajya Sangh (DGSS) led by Chandi Prasad Bhatt was at the forefront of this cooperative movement. Unlike the industries, these cooperatives were small-scale units involved in activities like resin distillation and making agricultural tools and bee boxes. What they really wanted was to use the forest resources sustainably and create jobs for local people.

In 1973, the DGSS asked the government for permission to fell a few trees from a forest near the Mandal village. They wanted to use the wood to make agricultural tools. The government refused to grant the permission. But shortly afterwards, it allowed a sports-goods company from Allahabad to fell a much larger forest area for wood to make cricket bats and tennis racquets!

The locals were enraged by the favouritism. On the day the sports-goods company came to fell the forest, they found members of the DGSS 'hugging' the trees to prevent them from being felled. In fact, that's how their movement got its name—'Chipko' is another word for 'hugging', in Hindi. Chipko quickly spread to other parts of the state. Ordinary villagers—men, women and children—took on powerful industries and stopped felling operations by hugging trees.

The Chipko movement received widespread publicity. Among the most famous images from it is groups of determined women holding on to trees.

One person who played an important role in popularizing the movement was Sunderlal Bahuguna. He walked close to 5000 kilometres across Himalayan villages, spreading awareness about the movement and gathering supporters. Bahuguna's long walk, similar to Mahatma Gandhi's Salt March, made him famous as the 'Mahatma of India's forests'.

Everyone has heard of Salman Khan, but not many know of the Bishnois. They're the people who sent him to jail for killing black bucks in their village near Jodhpur! For the Bishnoi tribe, killing animals and felling trees is a grave sin. In 1730, the maharaja of Jodhpur was building a new palace and needed wood. He sent his soldiers to cut down the Khejri trees growing near the Bishnoi villages in Jodhpur. When a Bishnoi woman, Amrita Devi, heard of what the soldiers were going to do, she ran to the spot and hugged the first tree just as the axe fell on it. She died on the spot. Hundreds of Bishnois from surrounding villages rushed to take her place and stop the men from chopping their trees. More than 350 were killed by the maharaja's men. The maharaja was deeply moved by the sacrifice of the Bishnois. He apologized for the actions of his men and promised that no Khejri tree would ever be cut and banned hunting near the Bishnoi villages. The words of Amrita Devi as she died have become a slogan for the Bishnois, 'A chopped head is . . . easier to replace than a chopped tree.'

The success of Chipko inspired a similar movement in Karnataka. The word for hugging in Kannada is *appiko*—and that's what the movement was very suitably called.

Is This a Forest?

With the industrial demand for raw materials picking up, existing forests began to fall short. They didn't have enough of particular trees, like pine, eucalyptus, teak and rosewood that were required by industries. So the government and industries began to replace natural forests with man-made ones by planting just the 'desired' trees. These man-made forests are also called monoculture or plantation forests.

If you're wondering, *what's the harm? After all they were planting trees*, think again. Just planting a tree is never enough. One has to think of many different things. For example, does the tree suit the type of soil and climate in a particular area? What of the animals and people living in the area? Will the tree that's being planted be useful to them?

A tree, plant or an animal that is naturally found in a particular area is called a 'native' species. It grows best in that area and helps the ecosystem. For instance, the Indian coral tree is native to many parts of India. Its lush red flowers are hard to miss between January and April. When in full bloom, many different birds such as crows, mynahs, babblers and parakeets, as well as bees and wasps swarm around it for nectar. The wide canopy of the tree offers shade to humans and animals in hot areas. Its protein-rich foliage makes for nutritious fodder and is also used to cure various infections and joint pain. During the dry season it sheds all its leaves to conserve water. These leaves form leaf manure that makes the soil fertile and is also used by farmers.

Indian coral tree

Unfortunately, few people thought of such things when natural forests full of different types of native trees began to be replaced by plantation forests. Most of these plantations were made up of fast-growing, high-yielding, non-native trees such as eucalyptus and acacia. They didn't suit the ecosystems within which they were planted and ended up creating trouble. For example, many environmentalists blame eucalyptus plantations for destroying the original habitat of the Nilgiri Tahr. Today, this goat—the state animal of Tamil Nadu—is an endangered species. The plantations also created a water crisis in several districts of Karnataka where they depleted groundwater and reduced rainfall. In 2017, the state officially banned the cultivation and propagation of eucalyptus trees.

Forest Pressures

The destruction of forests for industrial development doesn't end at plantations. Forests are also mined for coal and various other elements such as iron-ore and bauxite that are important for industries. They're submerged by dams and cleared to make more room for roads, towns, cities, factories and for agriculture. Natural and man-made fires also claim many acres of forest land every year.

Is It All Doom and Gloom?

The aim of successive governments since Independence has been to cover one-third of the country with forests. While we're still way off the mark, increasing environmental awareness has meant that we're working towards it.

Industrialization has firmly established the economic significance of forests. It has pegged a price tag to them. However, in the midst of pursuing the enticing monetary value of trees, we should not forget their environmental importance. Unthinkingly destroying natural forests or replacing them with plantations will help nobody in the long run.

It's also important to think about the people living in and around forests. The Forest Rights Act of 2006 finally granted these communities the right to settle in forested areas. However, ineffective implementation of this act has meant that their forest rights are still at risk. For these communities, the forest is their home and they often know it much better than anyone else. Instead of being left out, they should be actively involved in preserving India's forests.

A large number of people have devoted their lives to growing and preserving forests. Here are a few. Can you find out about others? Would you like to be like them?

In 1978, after giving his class 10 board exams, **Jadav Payeng**, a teenager from the Mishing tribe of Assam, returned to his village, Aruna Sapori. He had been away for many years, completing his schooling. When he came back that summer, he saw that the violent waters of the flooded Brahmaputra had washed up hundreds of snakes on its banks along his village—a large sandy island on the river. With no forest cover to shield them from the sun's heat and provide them food, the snakes had died.

JADAV PAYENG

Jadav was greatly distressed. He wanted to do something for the dead animals. The village elders advised him to grow trees. In 1979, when the local forestry division started planting a forest on the island, Jadav joined them. Unfortunately, the project was abandoned midway and everyone left. But Jadav continued growing the forest on his own. He released red ants, earthworms and termites into the soil. They churned it and secreted chemicals that increased its fertility. He built an irrigation system using earthen pots placed on bamboo platforms, from which water would drip down for days after a single session of watering.

Within forty years, he single-handedly grew an entire forest on his once barren island. It's full of bamboo, cotton trees, teak, custard apple, star fruit, gulmohur, tamarind, mulberry, mango, jackfruit, plum, peach, banyan, elephant grass and medicinal plants. Jadav's forest not only offers resources to the local community but also supports diverse wildlife—tigers, monkeys, snakes, deer, wild boars, birds, elephants and rhinos. In 2012, the Jawaharlal Nehru University in Delhi named Jadav the Forest Man of India.

SAALUMARADA THIMMAKKA

Jadav is not alone. There are many people across the country who are actively planting trees. In Karnataka, **Saalumarada Thimmakka**, who is more than 100 years old, has been planting trees since 1948!

If you take a trip from her village, Hulikal, to the neighbouring village of Kudoor, you will see close to 8000 trees that have been planted by her and her husband Bikkala Chikkayya.

SHUBHENDU SHARMA

Can growing a forest become a business? Yes, says **Shubhendu Sharma**, an industrial engineer who started a company called Afforestt in 2011 that grows dense, native forests to earn money.

7

Is Nuclear Energy Bad?

Between 1939 and 1945, the world was at war. One side was led by the USA, UK and the Soviet Union and the other by Germany, Italy and Japan. During the war, the USA secretly developed the world's first nuclear bomb. In August 1945, it dropped two nuclear bombs on the Japanese cities of Hiroshima and Nagasaki.

The Soviet Union was a group of countries comprising present-day Armenia, Azerbaijan, Belarus, Estonia, Georgia, Kazakhstan, Kyrgyzstan, Latvia, Lithuania, Moldova, Russia, Tajikistan, Turkmenistan, Ukraine and Uzbekistan.

The horrors of radioactive nuclear energy were unleashed upon Japan. The bombs ripped open the land and caused massive fires. Few living things—humans, plants or animals—survived for several kilometres around the bombed areas. A fearsome mushroom-shaped cloud formed in the air. It was so huge that it could be seen from space. Even though the war came to an end, countries across the world were frightened. What if a nuclear bomb had been dropped on them?

All chemical elements are made up of atoms and inside each atom is a nucleus, which holds large amounts of energy. This energy is called nuclear or atomic energy. Normally, nuclear energy is contained within the nucleus. However, in some elements, like uranium and plutonium, the nucleus is able to release or radiate this energy. These are called radioactive elements.

It was in this world, darkened by the terrifying power of nuclear energy, that India gained Independence. Non-violence had played an important role in our freedom struggle and we had a global reputation as a force for peace. Jawaharlal Nehru, the first prime minister of India, called the nuclear bomb a 'symbol of evil' and announced that India's nuclear programme would pursue the peaceful use of nuclear energy.

Homi Bhabha and the Pursuit of Nuclear Power

Nuclear physicist Homi Jehangir Bhabha was born in 1909 to a wealthy family in Mumbai. After completing studies overseas, Bhabha returned to India on a holiday in 1939. Just then, the war broke out and he decided to stay on.

Bhabha was a visionary and he had realized how useful nuclear energy

Homi Jehangir Bhabha

63

could be for powering India's industrial growth. In 1945, he founded the Tata Institute of Fundamental Research where initial research began on India's nuclear programme. After Independence, he convinced Nehru to set up an Atomic Research Centre at Trombay in Mumbai in 1954. It was renamed the Bhabha Atomic Research Centre (BARC) after his death in 1966. India also set up the Department of Atomic Energy, which would report directly to the prime minister.

BARC gave wings to India's pursuit of nuclear-powered electricity. The government began spending massive amounts of money on nuclear research and increased its efforts for international scientific collaboration.

In 1955, India achieved a major breakthrough in its nuclear programme when it managed to convince Canada to supply a powerful reactor. In 1956, the US chipped in and supplied heavy water—a form of water with atomic properties—for the reactor that came to be called CIRUS (Canada-India Reactor, US). India decided to mine and use its own reserves of the radioactive elements thorium and plutonium to fuel the reactor.

A nuclear reactor is a type of apparatus that uses radioactive fuels such as uranium and plutonium to produce heat that can be used for a variety of purposes, including generating electricity.

This collaboration happened long before there were any international treaties that regulated such technology transfers and provided for inspections to ensure peaceful use. By using its own fuel, India succeeded at keeping virtually complete control over CIRUS. It finally had the technology to process radioactive fuels and produce nuclear energy. It also used the design of CIRUS to make other, more powerful reactors. Nevertheless, at the time of the transfer, the understanding was that the reactor would only be used for peaceful purposes.

India's first nuclear power plant at Tarapur, near Mumbai, started operations in 1969. Today, it has more than twenty nuclear power plants.

Growing Tension

Even as India was working on the peaceful uses of nuclear energy, the world was becoming an increasingly insecure place. At the beginning of the 1960s, USA, Russia, UK and France had declared themselves as Nuclear-Weapon States. Calls were being made for nuclear disarmament—which means reducing or eliminating nuclear weapons—and different disarmament treaties were being signed.

Even though India supported nuclear disarmament, it didn't sign most of these treaties. It felt that they were unfair because they stopped Non-Nuclear-Weapon States from developing these nuclear weapons and put them at a disadvantage against the handful of Nuclear-Weapon States. Unless countries with nuclear weapons completely destroyed them, how could the rest of the world feel safe?

Smiling Buddha

In 1964, China successfully tested a nuclear weapon to become the fifth Nuclear-Weapon State. India felt unsafe—it had just lost a war against China two years ago. That's how India finally started developing nuclear weapons.

In 1970, the Treaty on the Non-Proliferation of Nuclear Weapons (NPT) came into force. Most countries, including all the Nuclear-Weapon States—USA, Russia, UK, France and China—signed it. It banned the spread of nuclear weapons and their technology. India caused an international uproar when it refused to sign the NPT.

A few years later, in May 1974, India tested its first nuclear bomb at Pokhran in Rajasthan. Raja Ramanna, who led a team of scientists at BARC to develop the bomb conveyed the successful testing to the then prime minister, Indira Gandhi, with a coded message: 'The Buddha is smiling'. That's how the test, officially called Pokhran I, came to be known as Smiling Buddha.

So, India had refused to sign the NPT *and* tested a nuclear bomb; the world was upset with it. In 1975, several countries got together to form the Nuclear Suppliers Group (NSG). It stopped the export of nuclear technology and fuel to countries like India that did not inspire confidence and subject their nuclear programme to inspections that ensured peaceful use.

In one stroke, India found itself isolated from the worldwide trade in nuclear technology and fuels. Its programme suffered a big setback without international help, but India didn't stop developing nuclear weapons. In May 1998, it declared itself a full-fledged Nuclear-Weapon State after detonating five bombs in Pokhran. Shortly afterwards, Pakistan also conducted its first nuclear tests. India was universally condemned for slapping efforts at nuclear disarmament.

The 2018 Bollywood movie *Parmanu* is a dramatized retelling of the 1998 blasts at Pokhran.

Civil Nuclear Deal

Even though India had become a Nuclear-Weapon State, it insisted on its peaceful intention and even adopted a no-first-use policy—it would only use its nuclear weapons in retaliation and would not use or threaten to use them against a Non-Nuclear-Weapon State.

Slowly, it managed to convince most countries that it meant well and was primarily interested in using nuclear energy for peaceful purposes, especially producing electricity. In 2008, the US signed a Civil Nuclear Agreement with India. This lifted the barriers imposed on India by the NSG. It could now access nuclear technology and fuel from the NSG in exchange for subjecting itself to inspections that ensured their peaceful use.

Safety Issues

Nuclear energy can be used peacefully, but it's hard to ignore its destructive power. Exposure to radiation from radioactive elements, especially uranium and plutonium, is the biggest danger. It can poison all humans, plants and animals coming in contact with it and lead to deadly diseases like cancer. What's even more alarming is that these elements can continue to emit radiation for hundreds of years, prolonging the damage.

One of the most famous victims of the 1945 bombings at Hiroshima was 2-year-old Sadako Sasaki. Although she survived the bombings, exposure to nuclear radiation made her very sick in the years afterwards. One day, a friend told her that if she made a 1000 paper cranes, her wish for better health would be granted. Sadako's determination to make the cranes made her a hero. If you ever visit Hiroshima, go to the Peace Memorial Park. There you will find a Children's Peace Monument, also called the Tower of a Thousand Cranes. It is dedicated to all the children, like Sadako, who died because of the bombings.

Even though nuclear weapons have never been used after 1945, accidents at nuclear power plants have made many people question the safety of nuclear energy and led to anti-nuclear protests around the world. One of the most famous anti-nuclear protests in India has been against the Kudankulam Nuclear Power Plant in Tamil Nadu.

Villages by the Sea

During the 1980s, India decided to build a nuclear power plant at Kudankulam, close to the sea coast in Tamil Nadu. However, people living around the plant, mainly fishing communities, were opposed to it. India had already suffered the Bhopal gas tragedy (*see page 82*) because of an industrial accident and in 1986, a massive explosion at the Chernobyl Nuclear Power Plant in Ukraine had raised global fears. How could the people trust that nothing would go wrong with the plant at Kudankulam? And if something did go wrong, they would end up suffering the most. They would not just risk losing their lives, but also their livelihood and their natural environment.

The protests became even more urgent in 2011 when a tsunami led to a devastating meltdown at the Fukushima Daiichi Nuclear Power Plant along the sea coast in Japan. Thousands of people living in the areas around the plant had to leave their homes. High levels of radiation were found in local food and water supplies and people were warned against consuming them. Even the seawater close to the site was contaminated and had to be pumped out as quickly as possible to prevent it from spreading. Japan, which had suffered the only nuclear bombings in history, acted fast to contain the devastation. But would India be able to do the same if something went wrong at Kudankulam?

In 2011, India passed its first nuclear liability law that defined who should be held responsible in the case of an accident and ways in which they would be punished and penalized. The following year, based on petitions submitted by the protestors, the Supreme Court made it clear to the government that it could not operate the Kudankulam plant without ensuring that all safety measures for handling disaster had been put in place. The government was also asked to submit a disaster management plan for the villages surrounding the plant and carry out mock safety drills, which were to be repeated every two years.

In 2014, the plant started generating electricity—more than a decade after construction began in 2002.

Is nuclear energy the same as energy drawn from eco-friendly, renewable sources like sunlight and wind? Technically, nuclear energy is renewable because nearly everything around us is made up of atoms and all atoms have a nucleus that contains nuclear energy. However, it's generally not included under renewable sources of energy because the Earth has a finite supply of radioactive elements, especially uranium, that are used to release nuclear energy.

So, Is Nuclear Energy Bad?

No one can deny the growing need for electricity. Thermal power plants that generate most of the world's electricity, burn fossil fuels such as coal and oil to boil water. Steam from the boiling water is used to turn turbines—large, wheel-shaped structures—that produce electricity. The release of nuclear energy also generates a large amount of heat, which can be used to boil water, turn turbines and produce electricity. Unlike burning fossil fuels, this neither pollutes the air with smoke nor does it release greenhouse gases that make the world warmer and lead to climate change. That's why nuclear power plants are considered a cleaner alternative to thermal power plants. Yet, they're not as widely used.

This is because even though nuclear energy is clean, it's not the safest. There is also the question of radioactive waste generated by these plants—how does one dispose it safely, so it doesn't pollute the environment? Moreover, reactors that are used to produce electricity can also be used to process nuclear fuel for weapons—that's why countries are wary of 'peaceful' uses of nuclear energy.

8

'Seeds' of History

Fruits, vegetables, pulses, cereals . . . almost all food comes from plants. From mighty elephants and tiny caterpillars to human beings, most life forms would starve without plants. In fact, the entire food chain would collapse. Plants aren't just a source of food but of oxygen too. Yet every time we talk of extinction, we almost always talk of animals, while thousands of plants are also vanishing from the Earth.

So, how do we save plants?

When You Sow a Seed...

When you sow a seed, you aren't just growing a new plant, you're also ensuring you have more seeds for the future. For example, if you sow a tomato seed and it grows into a tomato plant, you can get more seeds from the tomatoes growing on the plant. If you save and sow these seeds, you're doing what humans have been doing for thousands of years. After all, that's how we began growing our own food.

Seeds of plant varieties that have been saved and sowed again over a long period of time to produce similar plant varieties are called heirloom seeds. Till the Green Revolution, heirloom seeds were quite common in India. However, the seeds introduced in India during the Green Revolution (*see page 13*) changed Indian agriculture. Unlike heirloom seeds, these seeds could not grow well without using suitable chemical pesticides, fertilizers, irrigation and modern farm equipment. Moreover, they could not be saved and grown again like heirloom seeds. So farmers found themselves spending lots of money to grow these seeds. Still, they continued using these seeds because the yields were huge and demand was great—their produce would get sold in a jiffy!

By the 1980s though, some of this attraction started wearing off. In some places, the soil had lost its fertility and yield had started reducing because of all the changes and new diseases affecting the Green Revolution crops. This was a big blow, especially to farmers who owned small plots of land. Without enough yield, how would they recover the money they had spent on farming? What were they going to do?

The Seed Movement

The *Beej Bachao Andolan*—Save the Seeds Movement—started in India when farmers from Jardhargaon in Uttarakhand decided to go back to growing local crop varieties using traditional ways of farming.

Led by a fellow farmer and activist, Vijay Jardhari, they travelled all over their state in search of heirloom seeds of local varieties. By the end of it, they'd collected hundreds of heirloom seed varieties, including several types of rice and beans grown in the region. They also uncovered a remarkable system of traditional farming called *baranaja* in which twelve or more crops—a mix of cereals, lentils, vegetables—are planted together. The crops grow in harmony with each other and make the soil fertile over time. The produce isn't as high, but it's inexpensive because the farmers don't need to spend money on buying new seeds, chemical fertilizers or pesticides. Even under unfavourable conditions such as pest attacks or poor weather, the farmers usually manage to get enough produce to feed themselves, their families and their livestock.

The activists of the movement farmed the seeds they had found. They organized awareness campaigns, including meetings and marches, to discuss the benefits of traditional farming and local varieties with other farmers. They preserved and shared seeds with the community. Today, more than 30 lakh people in Uttarakhand practise baranaja and grow local varieties. Elsewhere too, in states like Sikkim and Kerala, farmers have turned to traditional farming and local seeds. The demand for such organic produce is growing and various movements like Navdanya also promote it.

Vijay Jardhari inspired farmers in Uttarakhand to return to traditional farming and local crops

Saving Crop Diversity

Did you know that rice can also be black and corn can also be red? Maybe not . . . That's because these varieties became rare in the aftermath of the Green Revolution, when more and more farmers started growing fewer and fewer varieties of crops. So, most rice grown today is white and most corn is yellow. The Food and Agriculture Organization estimates that more than 90% of crop varieties have disappeared from farmers' fields because hardly anyone is buying them. Unless the seeds of these varieties are saved, they'll become extinct.

Having as many varieties of a crop as possible is called crop diversity. Today, crop diversity is in danger not just because farmers are growing fewer varieties, but also because even the ones they are growing are threatened by diseases, pests and disasters such as droughts, cyclones, floods and war. The changing climate is making matters worse. There was a time when farmers could predict the changing of seasons. But today, strange weather is all over the news. Unseasonal rainfall is being witnessed around the world and every year India loses crores of acres of crops to it.

Unless we save seeds and preserve crop diversity, we may find ourselves in a future where there just won't be enough crops to feed and sustain all of humanity.

Seed Banks

Today, most countries around the world have banks that store a variety of seeds under special conditions, so they can be saved for long periods of time. These are called seed banks and they offer a backup against all the dangers threatening our crops. For example, after the 2004 tsunami, seed banks supplied paddy farmers in affected areas with seed varieties that could cope with changes in the soil condition.

The Svalbard Global Seed Vault, located on an icy, remote mountain in Norway, is the world's largest, and possibly, safest seed bank. It's also called the 'doomsday vault'. India has its own version of a doomsday seed vault at the Chang La mountain pass in Ladakh.

India has hundreds of seed banks, many of which were built after the Save the Seeds Movement. Most of them are community seed banks, operated by local people, that store seeds traditionally grown in the region. Farmers borrow these seeds and after harvesting the crop, return more seeds than they borrowed. For example, if a farmer borrowed a kilogram of cotton seeds, he would need to return one and half kilograms or more, based on the rules of the bank. Every bank keeps a record of borrowers, the seeds that were borrowed, the quantity that was borrowed and when it was returned. These seed banks, however, are very different from the one at Svalbard or Chang La. They're much smaller, hold a limited variety of seeds and are not usually built for long-term storage. India also has a national seed repository at the National Bureau of Plant Genetic Resources.

Farmers across the country take part in seed festivals, where they can exhibit and exchange local seeds. If you're interested in gardening, perhaps you can look out for these seeds at a festival happening in your city?

Make your own seed bank

- Select seeds—some banks keep seeds from around the world, others only keep local varieties. They carefully research the seeds before making a selection so they have a good mix of rare and popular varieties.
- Collect the seeds—when and how it's best to do this for a particular plant.
- Record details—for example, description of the plant, where the seed was collected, soil type, etc.
- Label or organize the seeds—so it's easy to retrieve them when needed.
- Clean the seeds—to save only a high-quality sample.
- Dry the seeds—to reduce moisture and get them ready for storage.
- Store the seeds—place them in sealed, airtight containers and keep them under suitable conditions, so they don't spoil and can be planted later.

Bt Cotton

In 2002, several decades after the green revolution, India introduced a new variety of seeds for growing cotton. These were called Bt Cotton seeds.

Cotton has always been a popular crop in India. Just have a look at your wardrobe—it is likely to have a large number of clothes made of cotton. However, the cotton crop is very sensitive to pests, especially the bollworm. The female bollworm lays her eggs inside round, fluffy clumps of cotton. When the eggs hatch, the new-born bollworms have a ready source of food. They eat up the seeds and damage the cotton as they burrow through it. To save their cotton crops from pests like bollworms, cotton farmers use a large amount of pesticides.

Every seed has hereditary units called genes. These genes 'instruct' the seed to grow into the plant from which it came. That's how a tomato seed grows into a tomato plant and not a brinjal or a chilli plant. Yet, the genes of the new tomato plant are not entirely similar to its parent. That's why there is no guarantee that the new tomato plant will look exactly like its parents or have tomatoes that look and taste the same. Any change in genes is called genetic modification. It happens naturally, but humans can make it happen too. Even the miracle seeds of the Green Revolution were genetically altered. However, the main difference in Bt seeds is that they are modified using bacteria—an entirely different species.

Bt Cotton was a genetically modified seed armed with genes that could resist pests like bollworms. Bt stands for *Bacillus thuringiensis*, a kind of natural pest-repelling bacteria that was used in creating these seeds. Many traditional farmers even use it in dried powder form as a pesticide. That's why farming seeds that are genetically modified using this bacteria, reduces the need for pesticides. It also leads to far greater yields as losses due to pests are minimized. No health hazards have been identified so far. In fact, more than 90% of cotton grown in India today is Bt cotton. Most likely, all your cotton clothes are made with it!

Yet, many people are worried. How would this unnatural modification affect the ecosystem within which these crops are grown, the farmers growing them and the people consuming them? And even though Bt seeds require less pesticides, they too have to be bought again. Yields may stagnate or reduce over time as crops encounter new threats. For example, in 2015, cotton crops in Punjab and Haryana were devastated by the whitefly, a pest that was immune to Bt.

So, What Is To Be Done?

Using heirloom seeds, building seed banks and genetically modifying seeds to make them more resistant to dangers like pests are all needed in the future to sustain the exploding human population. However, these measures alone may not be enough. Seeds need a suitable environment to grow. Protecting or enhancing them may not work if we keep polluting land, air and water, and contributing to climate change that is altering our environment in ways beyond our imagination.

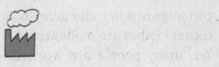

9

Nightmare in Bhopal

At 1 a.m. on 3 December 1984, a loud siren began to blow from the factory of the Union Carbide company in Bhopal. A foul smell filled the air. People woke up breathless. Their eyes and skin were burning as if someone had flung chilli powder on them. Many of them started vomiting. It had been nearly an hour since a deadly gas had started leaking out of the factory.

At the nearest hospital, the first patient was admitted at 1.15 a.m. A little over an hour later, there were 4000. The staff was shocked and bewildered. No one knew what to do. Soon, many of the staff members were also too sick to work. The hospital was crammed with patients. There were hardly any doctors and medicines began to run out.

At 3 a.m., a second siren began to blow. This one was much longer. But it didn't matter. By that time, there was

8000

The approximate number of people who died within days of the gas leak

already a stampede on the streets as hundreds of people desperately tried to escape the city. When morning came, death was everywhere—in homes, hospitals and streets.

The tragedy in Bhopal is often called the world's worst industrial disaster. But it was also a turning point in India's environmental history.

Making of the Disaster

The American chemical company, Union Carbide had set up the factory in Bhopal in 1969, to make pesticides for India's Green Revolution. These pesticides were made using a number of dangerous chemicals, including methyl isocyanate (MIC).

It's not unusual for a factory making chemical pesticides to work with dangerous chemicals. However, the factory in Bhopal wasn't safe. Workers complained about faulty equipment and poor operation and maintenance. Some had died in accidents inside the factory before. While these accidents had been controlled on time, no precautions were taken to ensure safety.

On the night between 2 December and 3 December 1984, disaster struck. Water accidentally leaked into a giant tank of MIC and set off a reaction that turned the chemical into gas. Dangerously high pressure began to build up inside the tank. Some workers thought something was wrong with the pressure-recording instruments. By the time they realized the enormity of the leak, it was too late. Many workers died inside the factory while a large cloud of the poisonous, heavy gas that had escaped, choked people living outside.

When MIC reacts with water at a high temperature, it can release as many as 300 poisonous chemicals. No one has been able to tell the chemical composition of the gas that escaped that night.

No one—neither the people nor the local government—knew what to do. They had dealt with natural calamities—floods and earthquakes—but they were completely unprepared for this. A factory using dangerous chemicals was operating close to them and yet no one knew much about the poison it had released or its antidote. Union Carbide did little to help.

The gas that had escaped took several days to dissipate. A lot of it dissolved in a lake surrounding the area. However, the horror wasn't over. Several tonnes of the deadly gas were still trapped inside the factory. So, at 8.30 a.m. on 16 December, a much-publicized operation was conducted to neutralize it. It was expected to end in four or five days but so much gas had been trapped that it took a week. Finally, Bhopal was gas-free, but it wasn't free from the effects of the gas.

Counting Losses

Thousands of people died of suffocation. But life was hell for those who survived. Exposure to the gas may not have killed them but it made them very sick. From breathlessness to eye pain, there seemed to be no end to their health issues. In later years, many developed deadly diseases like cancer. Children born to gas victims either died at birth or had birth defects. Many of these have been passed down through generations of the original gas victims. Even people who didn't feel as sick, found that they had lost their strength and could barely work. If they did, they would end up feeling ill. Labourers were the worst affected and often had to search for less tiring jobs.

Many studies were taken up to research the effects of the gas leak on the people and the natural environment. In 1985, the Indian Council of Medical Research (ICMR) began a study on the health impact of the gas on its victims. But it was left incomplete. So, there is no name for the disease caused by the gas, no identification of its victims or the status of their treatment. It's simply called the Bhopal Gas Disease.

It wasn't just people. Thousands of cattle and other animals were also killed by the gas. But there was no one to clear the carcasses since the municipal staff had also been affected. So, cranes, dumpers, sanitation workers from outside as well as the army had to be roped in to fix this issue. Within a few weeks, crores of green flies invaded the city, attracted by the improperly disposed carcasses. People feared that epidemics would break out because of poor waste management and sanitation. Even the green cover of the area was wiped out by the gas.

All the survivors were living in an environment that had been poisoned. The land they lived on, the air they breathed, the water they used, the fruits, vegetables and meat they ate—everything had been tainted by the gas. But it wasn't just the gas. The factory had been dumping tonnes of toxic waste in the area. A lot of it lay in the open, contaminating the soil and even seeping into groundwater in a few places. But the company neither cleaned the site nor warned people living around it about this danger. The factory had been a disaster throughout.

Make a Trip

In 2014, the Remember Bhopal Museum was opened in the city. It displays artefacts, oral histories, photographs, protest songs and campaign posters collected from a community of survivors and activists.

Changing Environmental History

The gas leak at the factory exposed the entire country to how poorly it was being operated and the terrible cost of such carelessness. Many victims were also disappointed by the government's inefficient handling of the emergency and distribution of compensation.

Union Carbide became infamous and was taken to court by the Indian government. The company settled the case in Indian courts by paying 470 million US dollars—much less than the original compensation claimed by the government. After that, it did everything in its power to dilute its responsibility in what had happened.

Many gas victims feel that justice was neither served to them by the company nor by the government. No one cared for their safety and when they fell in danger, they were not given enough help, especially compensation. Even today, many of them continue protesting for it.

The Bhopal gas tragedy opened India's eyes to the dangers of unsafe industrialization, especially factories working with hazardous raw materials. In 1986, India passed the landmark Environment (Protection) Act (EPA). Protecting and improving the natural environment and saving all living creatures including humans, plants and animals from hazards officially became the law of the land. Under EPA, the government made rules to close, prohibit or regulate any industry that had the potential to endanger the environment.

10

Gentle Giants

Elephants are the world's largest land animals and they need a large area to live freely—not just a forest, but entire landscapes or ranges with paths they can use to walk from one place to another in search of food and water. After all, their needs are also big. An adult Asian elephant can eat more than 100 kilograms of food and drink more than 100 litres of water in a day. Just one forest is not enough to meet these needs. That's why they walk hundreds of kilometres every year, allowing forests along their way to regenerate in time for them to return several months later.

In the first few decades after Independence, India was on a development drive. Land was cleared to grow crops, natural forests were replaced by plantations or mined to support industry, rivers were dammed, roads were built, factories, power transmission lines and railway lines were set up in more places and the human population began to explode. No one really thought about leaving room for elephants.

As their habitats were lost to development, cases of human-elephant conflict began to rise. Among the most common forms of this conflict was crop-raiding. Hungry elephants found an easy supply of food in farmlands. So, they

Engineering the Land

As herds of elephants travel from one place to another, they change the land. They dig it out and trample on it. They pull out grasses and knock down trees. When elephants clear out an area, they create room for more plants and animals to thrive on it. Seeds in their dung grow into new grasses, bushes and trees. Sunlight glows through the broken trees to reach the forest floor. Various animals, such as frogs and insects, take refuge under the fallen trees . . .

Watering Holes

Elephants can sniff out groundwater and use their feet, trunks and tusks to dig it out. These elephant-made watering holes provide water to all animals.

Poop Power

In a day, an elephant can poop out up to 50 kg of dung. Elephant dung is full of seeds from the plants it eats. It's also a great fertilizer. So, it not only disperses seeds, it also helps them grow. Many animals such as the dung beetle, even eat elephant dung! If you light up elephant dung, the fumes will drive away pesky mosquitoes. Some businesses even recycle elephant dung to make paper.

ransacked crops worth a lot of money and sometimes ended up injuring and killing villagers. In retaliation, angry villagers slaughtered elephants by poisoning or electrocuting them.

States found themselves struggling endlessly with this mammoth problem. Finally, in 1989, the central government set up a task force to look into the details of the problems being reported by different states.

Among other things, the task force found that elephants had disappeared from many places in which they were once found. It also noted that the wildlife reserves set aside during Project Tiger (*see page 42*) in 1973 were woefully inadequate for elephants. Conserving elephants meant that India needed to think big. In 1992, the government launched Project Elephant to save its gentle giants.

Saving Elephant Habitats

The task force had identified landscapes inhabited by elephants across India. These included the forest habitats of elephants, as well as corridors or routes they used to walk from one forest to another in search of food and water.

One of the first strategies of Project Elephant was to set aside forests in different landscapes as elephant reserves, fortified with plant varieties that could serve as food. It also sought to secure the corridors connecting these reserves to each other. The idea was to limit the need for elephants to venture into surrounding human habitats for food and water.

In 2001, Singhbhum in Jharkhand was officially declared the first elephant reserve of India. Sprawling over thousands of square kilometres across three south-eastern districts of the state, the reserve was part of an elephant range that also included other reserves in West Bengal, Odisha and Chhattisgarh.

Today, elephant reserves cover more than 65,000 square kilometres of forest land spread across eleven elephant ranges in different states in north-western, north-eastern, central and southern India. Meanwhile, more than 100 elephant corridors have been identified throughout the country with the help of the Wildlife Trust of India (WTI).

Unfortunately, less than 30% of elephant reserves and corridors fall within legally protected areas of India. This has made it easy for land in elephant ranges to be diverted for everything from mining and agriculture to building tourist resorts and constructing roads. More than 60% of elephant corridors have a national or state highway passing through them while about twenty of them have railway lines. Hundreds of elephants have been killed in train accidents over the years. One of the worst accidents took place in 2013, when a passenger train passing through the Chapramari Forest in northern West Bengal failed to apply brakes on time and rammed into a herd of elephants that were foraging near and on the tracks. Five adult elephants and two calves were killed while ten elephants were injured.

Various measures have been tried to prevent train accidents. These include reducing train speeds in elephant corridors and activating early warning systems. For example, in Tamil Nadu, sensors mounted on poles along the railway track monitor elephant movement. If an elephant sets off a sensor, a text message is sent to the railway staff and the animals are chased away. Railways have also experimented with some creative solutions such as devices that produce the buzzing sound of honeybees to keep elephants at bay. Long-term solutions include building overpasses or underpasses as safe crossing points for elephants, raising the railway track, or removing tracks from accident-prone areas.

> Researchers are puzzled about why elephants find themselves waiting on tracks even as they feel the vibrations of an approaching train. It could be that they get blinded by the train's light, especially at night, or they fail to spot trains coming around a curve.

A shrinking range, intersected by an ever-growing number of human settlements, farmlands, plantations, roads and railway lines, remains the biggest threat for elephants and a major reason behind human-elephant conflicts.

Human-Elephant Conflict

Reducing human-elephant conflict was a major objective of Project Elephant. Schemes were set up to pay farmers for loss of crops and families for loss of human lives. According to a WWF study, West Bengal, which has among the most stressed elephant populations in the country, spends the highest amount on controlling its elephants and the damage they cause. This works out to about 75,000 rupees for each elephant—one of the highest in the country. However, conservationists feel this system of doling out money is not helping. Instead, it's preventing locals from coming up with other ways to tackle the problem.

Barriers like trenches and electric fences have also been used to keep elephants away from cultivated land. Where such measures haven't worked, troublesome elephants have been captured.

Raiding a farm full of inviting crops like paddy, jackfruit or bananas may seem like an easy task for elephants, but it's not. For many elephants it's a risk. In fact, elephant herds with calves rarely raid crops because they're scared that this might endanger their young ones. So, who are these naughty elephants troubling farmers? Researchers believe it's usually the boisterous male teenagers who are not part of the herd.

In some cases, troublesome elephants have also been slayed. However, slaying elephants has been outlawed by India's Wildlife Protection Act and requires special legal permission. That's why, in many instances, locals have taken the law in their own hands and slaughtered troublemakers.

900

The approximate number of problematic elephants identified by the original Project Elephant taskforce

Early warning systems have been used successfully to alert locals about the presence of elephants. For example, in the Hassan district in Karnataka, if elephants are sighted, forest authorities use SMS alerts, automated voice calls and flashing LED lights at key public places to warn the locals. More than 35,000 mobile numbers are registered with them for this service and thanks to it, fatalities have been reduced to nearly zero.

In some places, conservation organizations have rehabilitated people away from elephant-infested areas. Awareness programmes have also been used to educate local communities on the benefits of elephant conservation.

Despite various measures, human-elephant conflict remains as tense as ever. It's estimated that 400 to 450 people lose their lives every year because of this conflict and about 100 elephants are killed to avenge the damage they cause.

One of the fallouts of this conflict has been a growing bitterness towards elephants. To counter this, India has taken steps like naming the elephant its National Heritage Animal, celebrating World Elephant Day on 12 August and launching campaigns like 'Haathi Mere Saathi' and 'Gaj Yatra'.

Poaching Elephants

Poaching elephants for ivory—the hard, white material that forms their tusks—has been a flourishing trade for centuries. Ivory is valued for its exquisiteness and has been a symbol of luxury through the ages. From artefacts and jewellery to weapons and musical instruments—it has been used widely.

Most of the ivory in the world comes from African elephants, because both genders have tusks. Among Asian elephants, only the males—also called bulls—have them. In fact, not even all males have them. Tuskless male elephants are called *makhnas*.

Import-export of ivory was banned in India in 1976. Ten years later, India also banned the domestic sale of ivory and products made from it. Despite this, hundreds of male tuskers were killed during the 1970s and the 1980s and Project Elephant found itself confronting this threat as soon as it was launched. In fact, the 1990s were one of the worst decades in the history of poaching.

Anti-poaching measures undertaken by Project Elephant included setting up patrols equipped with firearms and vehicles such as motorcycles, jeeps and power boats, strengthening communication systems like wireless sets, restoring forest roads for patrolling and establishing watchtowers.

The dreaded dacoit Veerappan terrorized forests in south India since the 1970s and poached hundreds of elephants for the illegal ivory trade. Veerappan's notoriety came to the government's attention  after his cruel killing of a range officer in 1987. This set off one of the biggest manhunts in India. Yet, it took more than fifteen years for him to be finally killed in 2004.

Fortunately, poaching appears to be reducing in India. According to the Wildlife Crime Control Bureau, more than 600 poachers had been arrested between 2008 and 2018, and the number of elephants poached had reduced from fifty-three in 2008 to just five in 2018.

Captive Elephants

India has a long history of capturing and taming wild elephants, which reached its peak during the Mauryan and Mughal empires. Rulers kept them in prime condition, especially because they were among the main war machines. Their imposing size instilled fear in the hearts of enemies. The Mughal emperor Akbar is believed to have had 32,000 elephants in his imperial stables and his son, Jahangir, a whopping 1,30,000. During British rule and for many years after Independence, elephants were also used for logging. Today, most domesticated elephants are used in tourism, such as elephant safaris, and during festivals and temple processions.

The demand for domesticated elephants has been falling and so has their number. In 2000, Project Elephant carried out a short survey of domesticated elephants, which revealed that India had at least 3400 such elephants. It was only in 2018 that the Supreme Court ordered the first ever census of captive elephants, which put their number at 2454. The highest number of captive elephants were in Assam, followed by Kerala, Karnataka and Tamil Nadu.

Although Project Elephant sought to improve the welfare of captive elephants by encouraging humane treatment, training keepers and boosting veterinary care, the protection of these elephants has largely fallen on the law. The Wildlife Protection Act and the Prevention of Cruelty to Animals Act protect captive elephants from brutality. Anyone possessing an elephant needs to have a valid certificate of ownership. Elephants cannot be captured from the wild, barring a few exceptions such as capturing troublesome elephants, and they cannot be sold.

Despite the legal protection, cases of inhuman treatment of domesticated elephants continue. This includes depriving them of sufficient food and water, confining or tying them in one place for long periods of time, beating and overly riding or loading them.

Counting Elephants

So how many elephants does India actually have? At the start of Project Elephant, India had about 25,000 elephants. However, each state used its own method of counting elephants and the numbers were not very reliable.

From 2002, India started conducting an elephant census every five years. The big difference was that states began to coordinate the counting, since elephants don't understand state boundaries and walk within ranges that extend into several states.

27,312

Approximate number of elephants in India according to the 2017 census

In 2012, India claimed to have more than 30,000 elephants but the last census, in 2017, reported a smaller number. This may be because counting has become more efficient with every census.

The 2017 census has been the most ambitious so far. Volunteers stationed in every five square kilometres of a particular forest did a simultaneous, direct count of elephants in their area. They also collected data on elephant dung in their area, counted waterholes and took pictures of elephants visiting them. All of this information across reserves was collated to determine India's elephant count.

Future of Elephants

The fight to protect elephants is essentially a fight over land and how much of it we're willing to leave for them. The quest for development has meant that more and more elephants find themselves with less and less suitable land. Yet, some remarkable work by conservationists under Project Elephant has meant that India continues to remain the home of the world's largest population of wild Asian elephants.

A large number of people have devoted their lives to elephant conservation. Here are a few. Can you find out about others? Would you like to be like them?

VINOD RISHI

As a teenager, **Vinod Rishi** went camping to the Rajaji National Park in Uttarakhand with his mentor Shri Nidhi, who wrote award-winning books on wildlife adventures. Rishi was petrified when a massive male tusker charged at them. However, his mentor merely raised his left arm and shouted 'Go . . . Go . . .' as loudly as possible at the charging elephant and took a few steps towards him. As it turned out, his mentor had been friends with the elephant who liked to stalk people and put on a frightening show before retreating! This encounter and others that he had while camping made Rishi a lifelong admirer of elephants. He went on to become a forest officer and the first director of Project Elephant.

In 1994, the prolific wildlife documentary film-maker **Mike Pandey** became the first Asian producer-director to win the Wildscreen Panda Award, also known as the Green Oscar, for his film *The Last Migration*. It captured human-elephant conflict in the forests of Surguja in Chhattisgarh. A decade later, he made its sequel

MIKE PANDEY

Vanishing Giants. Not only did it win yet another Green Oscar but it also sparked off a nationwide debate on the brutal capture of elephants and led the government to ban these methods that often ended up killing the animal. You can watch his movies on riverbankstudios.com.

Raman Sukumar is often called India's 'elephant man' and is one of the most definitive voices on the ecology of Asian elephants and human-wildlife conflict. In 1986, he helped set up India's first biosphere reserve—a significant ecosystem with

RAMAN SUKUMAR

a large population of elephants—in the Western Ghats. It has been declared a World Heritage Site by UNESCO. More than a decade later, he established the Asian Nature Conservation Foundation that promotes field research and conservation efforts to protect Asian elephants.

A co-founder of WTI, **Vivek Menon**, has played an important role in securing the future of Asian elephants in India.

VIVEK MENON

Decades of significant anti-poaching work, starting the first elephant rescue and reintegration centre in India, creating manuals on welfare in training and keeping captive elephants, and documenting and securing elephant corridors . . . he has spent a lifetime serving elephants.

11

A Yellow Taj Mahal

The grieving Mughal emperor Shah Jahan built the Taj Mahal as a symbol of love for his late wife Mumtaz. It was a monument so grand that even hundreds of years later we celebrate it as one of the greatest architectural wonders of our world. However, if Shah Jahan saw the Taj Mahal today, he might find his grief returning—despite all the adoration, his milky white monument, made of the finest marble, has turned a sickly yellow.

For many, the culprit is acid rain—a form of air pollution.

There's Acid in Rain?

When water evaporates, it becomes water vapour. Water vapour condenses in the air to form moisture, which comes back to earth in the form of rain. But what happens when water vapour mixes with polluting gases like carbon dioxide, sulphur dioxide and nitric oxide that are found in the air? We get acid rain.

Since there's so much carbon dioxide in the air, rainwater is usually full of carbonic acid. But carbonic acid is generally harmless. It's the sulphuric and nitric acid formed from sulphur dioxide and nitric oxide that make rainwater harmful. That's

because these acids are strong and can corrode things they touch. Every time we burn fossil fuels like coal or petroleum to run our cars, power stations and factories, more of these gases get released into the air, causing acid rain.

Even though acids can burn our skin, they're heavily diluted in rainwater. That's why we are unable to differentiate between acid rain and normal rain. Yet, it harms everything around us—soil, water bodies, plants and animals. It also corrodes man-made structures such as buildings and monuments, especially those made of marble and limestone.

Scientists began to study acid rain closely during the 1960s. By the 1970s, it had become one of the biggest environmental issues in the US. But it was not until 1990 that the US revised its law on clean air to specifically include the reduction of pollutants like sulphur dioxide and nitrogen oxides that cause acid rain.

Supreme Court to the Rescue

During the 1980s, the growing discolouration of the Taj Mahal caught the eye of a curious young lawyer, M.C. Mehta. He was told that this was happening because of acid rain, but he didn't know enough.

M.C. Mehta

Those were the days before the Internet. So, he spent a long time reading in libraries, making notes and seeking out experts to learn more about air pollution and its effect on monuments and the natural environment. In 1984, he

103

filed the first petition in the Supreme Court to safeguard the Taj Mahal. One of its main targets was an oil refinery, situated close to the monument, that spewed sulphur dioxide. Mehta argued that the monument was important to India's heritage and, as a tourist attraction, it contributed more to the country's economy than the refinery. He wanted all polluting industries around the Taj to either shut down, move out or use cleaner, non-polluting technology.

Twelve years later, the court ruled in his favour. An area of 10,400 square kilometres around the monument was set aside as the Taj Trapezium Zone (TTZ). Industries within the TTZ could not use fossil fuels like coal. Those that did had to close down, shift or switch to using natural gas. For many, it was a milestone in the environmental history of the land. The law had upheld the protection of the environment, people and cultural heritage from polluting industries.

Over the years, many other steps have been taken to protect Shah Jahan's legacy. For instance, since 2017, petrol and diesel vehicles have been banned within 500 metres of the Taj Mahal. The monument has even been given 'facials' using a type of clay called fuller's earth or *multani mitti* that soaks up impurities. Interestingly, it's also a popular beauty treatment for many women in the country.

So, Is the Taj Out of Danger?

Despite everything that's been done, the Taj Mahal's woes haven't disappeared. Acid rain may have corroded the marble, but many people believe it's not the only thing endangering the monument.

One of the biggest culprits is probably the city of Agra— where Shah Jahan built the Taj Mahal. Shah Jahan's Agra was a city of gardens lush with flowering bushes and fruit-bearing trees. A city where the Yamuna gurgled as it flowed through the land. Today, it's a city where lakhs of people jostle each other on the roads. Some walk while many drive around in polluting motor vehicles. The TTZ may have protected some areas, but pollution continues to haunt the city. Piles of garbage litter the streets, some from residents, some from tourists and some from the industries that have cropped up outside the TTZ. Once a gurgling stream, the Yamuna that flows through Agra is often nearly dry, and swamped with raw sewage. Insects that thrive in the dirt have been known to attack the monument, leaving green stains on it. Meanwhile, conservationists fear for the wooden foundation of the Taj Mahal, which needs moisture from the river to hold it in place. If the Yamuna dries up, it could sink the monument!

Yet, there are many who claim that worries over the future of the Taj Mahal are only a hype. For them, the Supreme Court's ruling has been a way of curbing businesses around the monument and ruining the local economy.

We all enjoy going on vacation. But tourism can have a negative impact on the environment, especially when the number of tourists is far greater than the ability of a place to provide for all of them. For example, trees may be chopped down to clear land for building more hotels and shops, tourists may use up large amounts of available resources such as food and water, and increase waste. Tourist vehicles may worsen air pollution. However, if it's managed sustainably, it can not only boost the local economy by providing jobs but also offer funds to preserve the local environment.

The Taj Mahal is not the only victim of environmental degradation, but its global popularity has made it a poster child for one of the many reasons behind why we need to save the environment.

Lotus Temple
It could turn 'grey' if it's not saved from Delhi's air pollution.

Charminar
Covered in layers of dust and is blackening and peeling because of the vehicles in its vicinity.

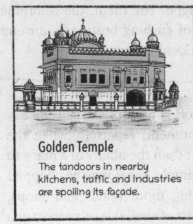

Golden Temple
The tandoors in nearby kitchens, traffic and industries are spoiling its façade.

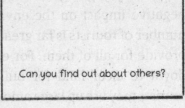

Can you find out about others?

Some other 'victims'

12
Uranium Poisoning in Punjab

In 2008, when South African medical expert Carin Smit visited the Baba Farid Centre for Special Children at Faridkot in Punjab, she was surprised. Children who were 3 years old looked like 7-month-old babies, 7-year-olds looked like they were only four and teenagers as old as sixteen looked like 8-year-olds. Carin had never seen such a disproportionate number of children with stunted growth and development anywhere. Something was very, very wrong . . .

Carin Smit

Carin specializes in auditory-integration training, a form of therapy for people suffering from hearing disorders. She is also a toxicologist—an expert on poisons—and she ventured a guess. Was it possible that all the children had been poisoned by something? At the time, it was just a theory. But she decided to test it by sending hair samples of the children to a laboratory. Luckily, a world-renowned German laboratory, Micro Trace Minerals, which works in the field of toxicity agreed to help.

Samples from 154 children were sent for testing. The results were received in 2009, and shocked everyone. More than 80% of the children had large amounts of uranium in their body—the same chemical element that is used in making nuclear bombs! It was so unbelievable that urine samples were collected to confirm the findings. But the results only got worse. The children had been poisoned not just by a heavy dose of uranium but many other toxic metals too.

From where were all these elements entering their bodies? The answer came soon enough. The groundwater in Punjab, which was not only irrigating its fields but also being used in its homes, had high levels of uranium and other toxic elements—something that had been researched and published a long time ago. Unfortunately, nothing had been done about it.

Carin's study broke the silence when it hit the news headlines not just in India but around the world. After that, several other studies confirmed the findings. Large areas of Punjab, the bread basket of India, were poisoned with chemical elements, especially uranium, which could lead to serious diseases, including cancer.

There is a train in Punjab called the 'cancer train'. Lots of cancer patients board this train from Bhatinda every day and travel all the way to Bikaner in Rajasthan to seek treatment at the cancer hospital there.

The Uranium Mystery

The biggest mystery in this issue was the source of uranium and other toxic elements. From where were they reaching the groundwater? Different people had different theories.

Punjab is an agricultural state and a lot of people wondered if the pesticides used in farming could be a source of the poison. Others thought it was coming from the waste created by the thermal power stations that burnt coal to generate electricity. While both of these did contaminate groundwater, they didn't offer an explanation for the uranium content.

One of the most plausible explanations relates to the natural occurrence of uranium in large areas of Punjab. Some researchers have suggested that when borewells are dug too deep to draw out groundwater, they hit the uranium-rich layer of the Earth. That's how the chemical enters the groundwater.

More than 10 years have passed since Carin's study exposed the toxicity in Punjab. But the only thing that people know for sure is that chemicals have poisoned the natural environment in Punjab and everyone—men, women and children—is suffering because of this.

In 1962, Marine Biologist Rachel Carson wrote *Silent Spring*, a book that shocked not only the people of America but also its chemical industry. From fish to birds and humans—the book claimed that the pesticide DDT was poisoning the entire ecosystem and even causing cancer. Powerful people in the chemical industry  attacked her. They questioned what she was saying and even called her crazy. Carson had expected such a reaction. So she supported what she was saying with no fewer than fifty-five pages of notes and a list of experts who had read and approved her book before it was published. Many renowned scientists supported her. When the then US president, John F. Kennedy ordered his Science Advisory Committee to examine the issues raised, Carson and her book won. A few years later, DDT was banned in the US. Unfortunately, pesticides like DDT continue to be used in India.

What Next?

In the aftermath of the exposé, the Supreme Court ordered the government of India as well as the state government of Punjab to take immediate action by cleaning up the state's groundwater.

But cleaning up such vast amounts of contaminated groundwater is not easy. Besides, the uranium that is removed must be disposed of properly, otherwise the problem may only increase. It might be better to stop digging wells too deep into the earth and over-exploiting groundwater.

A National Problem

Unfortunately, what's happening in Punjab is not an exception. Groundwater contamination is a nationwide problem. The Central Ground Water Board of India says groundwater in several Indian states is polluted with high amounts of chemical components like nitrates, fluorides, arsenic and lead. While some of these have seeped into the water when wells have been dug too deep, others have leached in from industries, landfills, chemical fertilizers and pesticides.

Groundwater is a major source of drinking water and irrigation in India. That's why polluted groundwater poses a huge risk to our health. Consuming it over long periods of time can lead to a variety of diseases. Hence, preserving and protecting its vital groundwater reserves has become an urgent need for India today.

In 2018, India began the five-year-long National Groundwater Management Improvement Programme. Only time will tell how successful it is at controlling contamination and boosting groundwater reserves.

13

India's 'Green' Court

What would you do to save a tree that's being chopped down in your neighbourhood? You could hug it and drive away the axemen like the *Chipko* movement revolutionaries. Or, you could ask them if they have legal permission to chop down the tree.

There are many laws that protect the environment in India, including several that prohibit the chopping of trees. Of course, there are exceptions. For example, a tree could be chopped if it's blocking a road and it's difficult to bypass, or if it's rotting and threating to fall down. However, before chopping it down, you need legal permission from the concerned government authority, such as the forest department or the Tree Authority. They will check the reasons behind why the tree is being chopped down. If they approve the chopping, they may also ask you to make up for the loss. For instance, they may order you to plant new saplings for every tree that is chopped down.

But anyone threatening to cut down a tree illegally can also be taken to the National Green Tribunal (NGT)—a court dedicated exclusively to cases related to the environment.

India was the third country in the world, after Australia and New Zealand, to have such a court.

How It All Started

Laws to protect the environment have been around in India since the 1850s, but during the 1980s, the Supreme Court expressed the need to have special environmental courts. It started with a case against a company in Delhi called Shriram Food and Fertilizers . . .

The industrial complex of Shriram Food and Fertilizers manufactured caustic chlorine and oleum. While many industries manufacture chemicals, the problem in this case was that the complex was surrounded by various thickly populated colonies, including Punjabi Bagh, West Patel Nagar, Ashok Vihar and Shastri Nagar, and was the source of heavy pollution.

In 1985, environmentalist and lawyer M.C. Mehta petitioned the Supreme Court, asking it to shut down and relocate the complex. Just a month after the petition was filed, oleum gas leaked out of the complex and into the surrounding colonies. One person died and some were hospitalized. Memories of the Bhopal gas tragedy (*see page 82*) were still fresh in people's minds and the gas leak got everyone very worried. The local administration rushed in and ordered the factory responsible for the leak to shut down. The company challenged this order in court while the victims filed for compensation.

In 1986, the Supreme court announced its verdict. It held the company responsible for the accident and asked it to compensate the victims. Even though industrialization was important, the court felt that any enterprise working with dangerous substances had an absolute responsibility to ensure the safety of the public and needed to take all steps to prevent any accident. If an accident occurred, it would be held solely responsible.

This judgement along with various others that the court passed on environmental issues in the following years, made it clear that such cases required technical expertise, prompt disposal and continuous monitoring. That's why it decided that such cases should be handled by courts that specialized in these matters and the National Green Tribunal was formed in June 2010.

How would you judge a case involving air pollution from a factory? How would this case be different from one that involves a kidnapping or a robbery? What would you need to know to arrive at a decision? How would you go about finding the facts? What would happen if your case is taking time while the factory continues operating? If the factory is guilty of causing air pollution, how would you penalize it and ensure that the offence isn't repeated?

Fast Facts About the NGT

The NGT is made up of people with a legal background as well as those with expertise on environmental issues. It's a fast-track court, which means that it decides on matters much faster than regular courts. However, if someone is not satisfied with its decision, they can take the case to other courts.

Can you take all environmental cases to the NGT? Not exactly. The tribunal currently deliberates only on certain cases, such as those involving air and water pollution, forest conservation and providing relief to victims of industrial accidents involving hazardous substances. So, if someone is chopping down trees or polluting a lake near your house, you could approach the NGT. But, if you discover an illegal wildlife racket involving the smuggling of animals or their body parts, the NGT will not be able to take your case and you will have to go the other courts in the country.

The NGT punishes polluters in several ways. For example, it can issue fines, impose bans, direct the demolition of unauthorized structures and order compensation for victims.

Since its foundation, the NGT has handled thousands of cases. In its pursuit of environmental justice, it has also taken up cases based on issues raised in newspaper articles and letter petitions.

Even though the NGT is not as powerful as the regular courts and may not be able to take on all environmental cases, it has helped in reducing the burden of regular courts. Many times, when polluters have challenged the NGT's judgement in the Supreme Court, the court has decided to stick with the NGT's ruling because of its legal as well as scientific basis.

The birth of the NGT was a milestone in India's environmental history. It is proof of the country's decision to uphold environmental justice.

Some Landmark Verdicts of the NGT

Plastic ban: Thanks to the NGT, many states in India have imposed either a complete or partial ban on plastic bags.

Ban on old vehicles: In 2018, the Supreme Court upheld the NGT's verdict that banned petrol vehicles older than fifteen years and diesel vehicles older than 10 years from plying on the streets of Delhi NCR, because of the pollution they cause.

Stubble burning: In 2015, the NGT imposed fines ranging from 2500 to 15,000 rupees on farmers burning stubble after harvesting crops. It also asked Delhi, Rajasthan, Punjab, Haryana and Uttar Pradesh to keep it informed about what they were doing to curb this harmful practice.

Can you find out about more cases? You can begin by visiting https://greentribunal.gov.in.

14

Mountains of Waste

Every year, Indian cities generate more than a whopping 6 crore tonnes of garbage. That's more than 60% of India's waste. Most of it ends up in open, unregulated landfills—large pits in which garbage is buried. Landfills are among the oldest, easiest and cheapest ways of waste disposal in the world and they've been swallowing a majority of our solid waste since long before Independence. Unfortunately, many of them are now fully saturated. So, instead of being buried in the ground, the garbage at these landfills piles up in huge mountains. If you cross Ghazipur in Delhi, you'll see India's tallest mountain of garbage—it's nearly as tall as the Qutub Minar!

Ticking Time Bombs

In January 2016, people in Mumbai woke up to the horrible smell of burning garbage. The city's oldest and largest landfill at Deonar was on fire. The raging firestorm was so big that it lasted over a week and could even be seen from space. The smoke enveloped the entire city for a long time. Pollution levels were so high that it was difficult for people to breathe

and schools had to be shut. Even though this was one of the biggest accidents at the landfill, it was neither the first, nor the last.

Many of India's landfills are ticking time bombs, where accidents like fires are common. Even the Ghazipur landfill has caught fires several times. What causes the fire? Rotting garbage at the landfills releases methane, a gas that catches fire when exposed to hot air. Apart from fire, these landfills also pose the threat of waste leaching into the soil and polluting groundwater.

Most developed countries stopped using open, unregulated landfills in the 1960s because of the dangers they pose to the environment and human health. Many switched to sanitary landfills where the bottom is lined with thick plastic and clay to prevent waste from leaching into groundwater. Each layer of garbage is covered with soil to allow it to decompose rapidly and once the landfill is full, it's sealed and covered with a thick layer of clay. Quite often, it's evaluated for safety and converted into a park or an open space for human use.

Unfortunately, suitable land is so hard to find in overcrowded Indian cities that existing landfills continue to be used well past their life and turn into unsightly mountains. For example, the Ghazipur landfill was established in 1984 and was saturated by 2002. Still, the city of Delhi continues dumping large amounts of its garbage in the landfill every day. In 2017, a portion of the landfill collapsed, sweeping away a car and three two-wheelers, killing two people and injuring five.

In many ways, the story of exploding, hard-to-retire landfills is a story of India's exploding, unplanned cities.

Make a Trip

If you happen to visit Chandigarh, drop by the Rock Garden. Created by Nek Chand in 1957, it's an epitome of how garbage can be used creatively. Sculptures in the garden are made using everything from broken bangles, ceramic pots, tiles and glass bottles to discarded plugs. It's perhaps one of the first such uses of waste in our country.

You can also plan to trip to Mawlynnong—Asia's cleanest village. This tiny hamlet in Meghalaya, with a little over ninety houses and around 500 people has 100% literacy. Everyone in the village is engaged in agriculture. Garbage is collected in bamboo bins and most of it is recycled and converted into manure that is used in agriculture.

Urbanization in India

Some of independent India's biggest cities such as Kolkata, Delhi, Chennai and Mumbai came up under the British empire. For example, in 1668, the Portuguese handed over an area to the British East India Company that grew into modern Mumbai. At the time, the city's population was just 10,000. Within the next seven years it reached 60,000. Today it's the most populous city in the country with more than 2 crore people living in it.

To manage the daily affairs of growing cities, the British set up municipal corporations. The first of these—the Madras

Municipal Corporation—came into existence in 1687. Even after Independence, when urbanization exploded and cities started getting overcrowded, these age-old municipal corporations have continued managing their local affairs. Unfortunately, they've often not been able to deal with the monstrous amounts of garbage, one of the many fallouts of uncontrolled urbanization.

Waste management has hardly figured in independent India's growth story. Back in the 1950s, we were pressed with so many big problems like hunger and maintaining communal harmony that it was considered relatively trivial. Most of the country resided in villages. Half of our waste was organic and the rest was ash, sand and grit. Nearly everything was easily reusable and recyclable. However, in 1991, India's economy changed in a big way and business prospered like never before.

Do you know one of the signs of prosperity? The increasing contents of your dustbin. The more you prosper, the more you can afford to consume and the more you consume, the more waste you generate. For example, it's very common for us to buy a bottle of packaged water when we travel today. But before 1991, this was hardly the case. People usually travelled with their own bottle of water and it was rarely sold the way it is today. So, there were nearly no disposable plastic bottles in our dustbin before 1991.

After 1991, India began to grow in a big way and its dustbins started overflowing with all manner of things—from empty bags of potato chips to disposable syringes and smartphones.

Plague in Surat

In 1994, the city of Surat in Gujarat suffered constant rain and floods for over two months. Drainage systems clogged up and the city was waterlogged. The municipal corporation failed to clean up the filth on time and a deadly plague broke out in the city. This was one of the first casualties of poor waste management in India post 1991.

At this point, India did have some rules about the disposal of biomedical and hazardous waste. But the plague led to a petition being filed in the Supreme Court to draw its attention to poor solid waste management in Indian cities and the failure of municipal corporations. The first major rules on solid waste management were passed in 2000. While the problem had been recognized by the law, it would take more than a decade for 'Clean India' to hit the national limelight.

Towards the end of the 1990s, India started a campaign to discourage open defecation and promote a cleaner environment. This transformed into the Swachh Bharat Abhiyan of 2014 when we went on a massive toilet-building spree and cleanliness became the order of the day. Brooms became the weapon of choice as everyone from the prime minister to movie stars got photographed sweeping the streets. Waste management laws were strengthened and everyone started talking about littering as a sin. Yet the problem of our landfills has continued. So, what's going wrong?

Did you know that Mahatma Gandhi was one of the first waste-warriors of India? From the very beginning, he emphasized that the need for sanitation and cleanliness was as important as winning freedom from the British. So it's no surprise that the Swachch Bharat Abhiyan used the iconic image of his spectacles as its logo.

India's garbage mountains won't go away till we keep heaping all our waste on them. Today, more than half the garbage that's collected is simply dumped in landfills. Just about 20% is segregated and recycled. This is an unorganized business involving *kabadiwallas* and ragpickers, who endanger themselves sorting through our garbage. We need to take a careful look at our dustbins to segregate and recycle more, so that very little of our garbage actually ends up in landfills. The good news is that this is not as hard as it seems because a lot of our

Looking inside our dustbins

garbage is either organic or recyclable. So, we can think of solutions like composting organic waste to make manure or recycling waste to create something useful, for example, pen-holders made from plastic bottles. There are tonnes of videos available online today that teach you how to make useful things from waste.

Plastic Problems

When plastic was invented during the 19th century, it was seen as a wonder material that could be used to cheaply produce durable goods. Nobody was really thinking about the big problem—plastic is so durable that it takes hundreds of years to decompose. So, even if you throw away plastic, it will keep lying around for a long, long time. Today, the world is nearly sinking in plastic waste—most of which has been created since 2000.

The plastic industry in India took off in the 1950s and has grown rapidly since then. Today, the average Indian uses about 11 kilograms of plastic in a year—a lot of it in the form of the common plastic bag. This is not a large amount compared to many developed countries, but given our huge population, it amounts to hundreds of kilo tonnes every year. In fact, India is among the top twenty plastic consuming nations of the world.

However, in 2018 the government declared that it will work towards phasing out all single-use plastic such as plastic bottles holding less than 200 ml of a beverage, thermocol, straws and plastic earbud sticks, by 2022. Many Indian cities have imposed a strict ban on single-use plastic. For example, in Mumbai, people caught with single-use plastic can be fined up to 25,000 rupees and jailed for up to three months.

Recycling plastic is also gaining momentum. In fact, according to a report from the Plastindia Foundation, the country recycled about 60% of its plastic waste in 2017–18. While this is good news, it's also true that plastic cannot be recycled more than five to seven times and does eventually end up as garbage.

India has also been experimenting with innovative uses of discarded plastic. For example, in 2015 the government made it compulsory for all road developers to use plastic waste for road construction. Since then the country has built about 1 lakh kilometres of roads using discarded plastic.

Today, like a lot of other countries, India is also experimenting with biodegradable plastic that breaks down in weeks or months instead of years. However, only time will tell how successfully we're able to use it.

Professor **Rajagopalan Vasudevan** is a chemistry professor who came up with the idea of using plastic waste in building roads back in 2001. He is also known as the Plastic Man of India.

RAJAGOPALAN VASUDEVAN

Several developed countries such as the US and many in the European Union export their plastic waste instead of recycling it themselves. Doing this is cheaper and far more convenient. Meanwhile, importing this waste is a source of income for developing countries. But, as waste piles up across the world, many 'importers' have started making a noise. In 2018, China stopped importing waste and in 2019 India did the same. Philippines even threatened to declare war on Canada unless it took back its garbage comprising household and electrical waste that had been labelled as plastic waste.

E-Waste

The electronics industry started in India during the 1960s. But it tended to focus on industries, space and defence. It was only in the 1980s that electronic devices like personal computers started picking up. After the internet appeared in 1994, there was no turning back and electronics propped with the power of the internet eventually took over the world.

In July 1995, Jyoti Basu, the chief minister of West Bengal made the first mobile phone call in India. From his office in Kolkata, he called and spoke to Sukh Ram, the Communications Minister in the Prime Minister's Office in Delhi.

By the 2000s, Information Technology (IT) began to grow rapidly in India, creating not just jobs but also users. However, the growing use of electronics also led to growing electronic waste. Today, India is the fifth largest producer of e-waste in the world, most of which comprises personal devices like mobile phones and computers. This is the latest waste problem gripping our country and it remains to be seen how we deal with it.

Waste-to-Energy

During the 1980s, India began to experiment with burning waste in incinerators and using the heat generated to produce electricity. It seemed like a great idea—it would not just reduce the pressure on landfills but also help in producing electricity. In fact, many countries in the west have used it extremely successfully.

However, Waste-to-Energy (WTE) plants are not an easy replacement for landfills. They're extremely expensive to operate and countries that have used them successfully use them hand-in-hand with segregation and recycling. They do not simply dump all their waste, including biodegradable waste, in these plants instead of landfills.

Burning waste releases toxic gases. Advanced WTE plants filter their emissions to reduce air pollution. They also recycle the by-products of waste incineration. For example, metals are extracted from the ash and reused, while the ash itself may be used in road construction.

Today, India has more than ninety WTE plants that can generate hundreds of megawatts of electricity. In fact, if they function well, they will be able to meet the energy requirements of entire cities. That's why the government has been trying to promote these plants.

However, this model doesn't seem to have worked successfully in India. A lot of these plants lie defunct. In many instances, residents oppose them because of concerns around air pollution and toxic ash. Experts claim that without effective segregation and recycling, WTE plants will not work in India. For example, a large amount of our waste is biodegradable and such plants function best with non-biodegradable waste. If unsegregated, mixed waste is emptied into them, they will use up more fuel to burn it. If emissions aren't filtered well, they will cause high amounts of air pollution and if the ash they generate is dumped into landfills, it will only pile up as toxic waste. Moreover, the power produced is also much more expensive than other sources.

So, What Do We Do About Our Waste?

There are no easy solutions to waste management. Most major cities around the world have taken centuries to change before becoming the clean cities of today. This involved a strict enforcement of laws that made cleanliness a way of life.

Think—will you litter in a place if you're scared of being caught and punished for doing so? Or if you worry about being seen as a 'dirty litterbug' because everyone else follows the laws of cleanliness? Managing waste is a complex idea that needs strict enforcement as well as a change in mindsets.

However, a big positive development has been that a lot of organizations have sniffed out a huge business opportunity in waste management. From offering services to collect, segregate and recycle waste to organizing zero-waste social functions like parties and weddings, and selling an array of things like stationery, shoes, bags and jewellery made from waste, they're inspiring India to embrace its garbage and turn it to gold.

An Example for the World

Sweden is one of the champions of waste management. Residents segregate their waste and most of the non-biodegradable waste is sent to WTE plants where it's used to produce electricity, while the rest is converted into bio-fertilizer and biogas. Less than 1% of it ends up in landfills. In fact, Sweden has become so good at recycling that it even imports about 8,00,000 tonnes of waste from other countries to feed its WTE plants. This is why it is not just a zero-waste but a negative-waste country.

15

Not a Drop to Drink

Chennai, the capital of Tamil Nadu, is one of the largest cities in India. But this large city has a larger problem—hardly enough water! Even though water crisis had hit smaller Indian cities such as Latur and Shimla in the past, on 19 June 2019, Chennai became the first big city to declare a water emergency. The city had run out of most of its potable water and called it 'Day Zero'.

However, more than 70% of our planet is covered in water and Chennai is right next to the sea, then how did it run out of water?

Most water found on our planet is too salty to use. Just a little over 2% of it is usable. The water we can use, especially for drinking, is freshwater—which has little to no impurities such as salts or solids dissolved in it and comes from the Earth's atmosphere, in the form of rain, snow and mist.

Freshwater is one of our most precious natural resources. It fills our rivers and reservoirs. It also seeps into the ground to fill up underground aquifers, where it's stored as valuable groundwater. From these rivers, reservoirs and underground aquifers, it comes to our homes, farms, offices, hospitals, schools, colleges and factories, where we use it for everything from drinking to irrigation and lots more.

India has about 18% of the world's population and about 4% of its freshwater. Is that why it's running out of potable water? No, India's water crisis isn't about having insufficient water. There are many other reasons behind it and most of them come together in Chennai.

Chennai's Dilemma

Climate change has been making the rainy season unpredictable over large parts of the world and Chennai is no exception. In 2017 and 2018, the city didn't receive enough rainfall. However, there had been many heatwaves during this period. The city's underground aquifers were parched and the four reservoirs—Poondi, Chembarambakkam, Cholavaram and Red Hills (or Puzhal)—supplying more than half its water had dried up. That's why it had to declare Day Zero and spend crores of rupees to have trains bring in lakhs of litres of water from Jolarpettai, a small town located over 200 kilometres away. The neighbouring state of Kerala also 'donated' lakhs of litres.

So, is climate change responsible for Chennai's woes? Scanty rainfall and intense heatwaves dried up its reservoirs and aquifers and that's why the city ran out of water, didn't it? Not really. Climate change was only part of the problem. However, the crisis was largely man-made.

120th out of 122: India's rank in the water quality index. More than 70% of our water is contaminated and most households don't have drinking water!

120th

60 CRORE

The number of people who face high to extreme water stress in India

2,00,000

The approximate number of people who die every year because of the use of contaminated water

40%: Population that may not have access to drinking water by the year 2030

84%: Rural households that don't get piped water. In fact, women in many parts of rural India walk hundreds of kilometers a year just to fetch water.

Watery Facts, Source: Niti Aayog, 2018

Meghaa Gupta

Making Room for People

The modern city of Chennai grew out of Fort St George—a unique fortified settlement built by the British East India Company in the 17th century. At the time, it just had a few thousand people. Today, the population is more than 1 crore. But this expansion came at big price—water bodies and wetlands were filled up to make room for people to stay, roads for them to travel on, schools and colleges for them to study in, offices and factories for them to work in . . . Once upon a time, Chennai had more than 600 water bodies, including big lakes and storage tanks. By 2017, it had less than thirty! Even the wetlands in and around the city have shrunk to less than a tenth of their original extent.

If you live in Chennai or happen to visit the city, pay attention to the names of the roads. Some of them, like Tank Bund Road and Lake View Road are actually named after waterbodies that used to exist in the area a long time ago.

The people who were planning and building the city didn't think of one key element—where would they get water for so many people if they kept destroying waterbodies and wetlands?

Neither did they pause to wonder where all the rainwater would go if there weren't enough waterbodies and wetlands to collect and store it. In 2015, it rained so much that the city nearly drowned! There was no place for the water to go and it couldn't seep through all the concrete. So, it flooded the streets. Boats were plying on some roads. When the sun came out, most of the water evaporated.

A River Is Dead ... Long Live the River

Chennai has three main rivers—the Kosasthalaiyar to the north, the Cooum in the middle and the Adyar river to the south. During the 19th century, the British connected all the three rivers with the Buckingham Canal for ease of navigation. The rivers are seasonal and depend heavily on rainwater.

But since the 1960s, these rivers have been getting gradually swamped by garbage and sewage from the city's growing commercial establishments and residential areas. Even the canal is choked. When it doesn't rain, the rivers hardly flow. When it rains, dirty rainwater from the streets drains into them, adding to their woes. When it rains too much, they flood the city with their dirty water. The water flowing through these rivers has been gradually laid to waste.

Meanwhile, the reservoirs are not completely cleared of silt, so they're not able to store as much water as they should.

India is the second most populated country in the world. Can you guess the biggest contaminator of water? Our poop!

Drill, Drill, Drill a Hole

Like a lot of other cities in India, Chennai has also relied heavily on groundwater through a lot of its history. In the early 1750s, groundwater in the wells at Fort St George turned salty because of overdrawing. So, the British scouted for available resources and dug seven more wells that supplied water to the fort through pipes. This was the first organized drinking-water system in the city and among the earliest piped-water systems in the country. These wells supported a growing city for many years, before twenty-seven more wells were dug up in 1818. Relying on underground wells went on till the 1860s, when a check dam was constructed on the Kosasthalaiyar river to divert its water to the Red Hill reservoir, designed to supplement the city's water supply. Yet the demand of its ever-expanding population has exceeded supply and the city is nearly out of groundwater today.

Water is such a precious resource that it has long featured in wars and fights. During the 18th century, Chennai faced many intruders. One of them, Hyder Ali, the ruler of Mysore, tried to poison its wells with animal carcasses, but they were so well-protected that his plans were foiled!

Let's Catch the Rain

So Chennai has too many people, and its reservoirs, underground aquifers and dirty rivers are failing to keep up with their need for water. The obvious solution to water crisis is conservation. One of the oldest ways of conserving water is rainwater harvesting—collecting and storing rainwater so it can be used later.

Stepwells are among the many ways in which rainwater has been harvested in India down the ages. A stepwell stores large amounts of rainwater that people can fetch by climbing down steps that are cut into its sides. Stepwells are called by different names in different places. For example, they're called 'vav' in Gujarat and 'baolis' in Rajasthan.

If you turn the purple 100-rupee notes issued in India in 2018, you'll find a picture of the Rani-ki-Vav (the Queen's Stepwell)—one of the finest and most elaborate examples of stepwells in India. Built during the 11th century AD in Gujarat, it's designed in the form of an inverted temple with seven levels of stairs featuring artistic sculptural panels. In 2014, it was recognized as a world heritage site by the UNESCO.

Even though many of these traditional ways of harvesting rainwater were lost in time, the practice has picked up again. In fact, Tamil Nadu was among the first states to make rainwater harvesting compulsory for every building. The state government had passed the order after a particularly bad drought in the early 2000s. Unfortunately, it was poorly implemented and that's why, many believe, Chennai reached Day Zero.

My Friend, the Sea

So, what can a city do when it's running out of freshwater? Can it turn to the sea for help? Even though seawater is too saline to use, humans have long made efforts to obtain drinking water from the sea—after all, it is the most abundant source of water on the planet . . .

Not surprisingly, among the first people who tried getting drinking water from the sea were apparently sailors on ocean ships. However, it was not until the 20th century that factories that could remove salt from water on a large scale appeared on the scene. These factories or desalination plants usually use Reverse Osmosis (RO), in which seawater is passed through a series of membranes with increasing force. This removes salt and other impurities including bacteria, making the water fit for human use.

The first and one of the largest desalination plants in India came up in 2010, at Minjur in Chennai. Currently, it can desalinate about 10 crore litres of seawater a day. While this adds to the city's water reserves, it may not be the best solution because of how expensive this process is. Moreover, such plants flush out extremely salty brine back into the sea, which is harmful for marine life.

Seeing the Wealth in Wastewater

The idea of treating wastewater from homes, offices and factories in sewage treatment plants before sending it into waterbodies is an old one. The first wastewater treatment plant in the world came up in Japan, back in 1922. Chennai, which started treating its wastewater during the 1970s, was one of the first cities in India to do so. Unfortunately, treatment hasn't kept pace with the amount of wastewater that the city has been generating. If it did, the Adyar, Cooum and Kosasthalaiyar rivers, as well as the Buckingham Canal would not have been as dirty as they are.

Treating wastewater though, is not the end of the story. What if we use it again instead of sending it into our waterbodies? Scientists say wastewater is mainly water. Only a small percentage of it contains pollutants. So, when we allow it to drain out of the water supply, we're actually wasting large amounts of water. For a water-stressed city, this is a very bad idea. So, in 2019, Chennai announced that it would start diverting wastewater from some of its treatment plants for industrial use. If this plan succeeds, Chennai would become the first big city in India to reuse about 20% of its wastewater.

However, setting up a plant and treating water is much more expensive than just letting it flow untreated into waterbodies. Besides, not all parts of our country even have a sewerage system with pipes and drains to carry wastewater. For instance, in urban areas that are responsible for a large chunk of wastewater, only about 3.3 crore out of 10 crore households are plugged into a sewerage system.

Who are the manual scavengers we keep reading about in the news? They're people who clean blocked sewers on our roads—manually removing the filth. To do their work, they often need to climb down sewers that are full of poisonous gases being released from the waste. It's risky work and the danger increases because the workers are not adequately protected. Many use their bare hands to clean the sewers! In 1993, India banned the employment of people as manual scavengers and in 2013, it passed a law prohibiting manual scavenging in all forms. Unfortunately, nothing has been able to end this practice completely.

Not Just a City

Chennai may have a lot of problems, but it's not the only city with a water crisis. In a 2018 study by the World Wildlife Fund for Nature (WWF), four Indian cities featured among top twenty megacities around the world facing a severe water crisis. While Chennai topped the list, Kolkata came in second, Mumbai was at number 11 and Delhi at number 15.

Racing for water

Gurugram (formerly Gurgaon) used to be a sleepy agricultural town surrounded by muddy ravines and waterbodies. But its closeness to Delhi led to a boom that saw the rise of the swanky Gurugram of today, that has offices of some of the biggest companies in the world and buildings that run into several floors. But even as Gurugram made room for roads and buildings, like Chennai, it destroyed nearly 250 of its 300 waterbodies. Neither did it think of viable, well-maintained sewerage systems. That's why, just a few millimetres of rain end up flooding its roads every year.

Rivers and waterbodies across the country are polluted. The plight of the Ganga, India's longest river that passes through more than thirty cities, seventy towns and thousands of villages, is an example of how river conservation seems to be failing in our country. During the 1980s, India initiated the Ganga Action Plan to clean up the river. But more than twenty years later, despite spending thousands of crores, the river remains dirty. Meanwhile, domestic and industrial waste dumped in India's lakes has meant that many of them, like Bengaluru's infamous Bellandur lake, perpetually catch fire.

But not all is lost. Rainwater harvesting has become mandatory, especially for new buildings, in most cities of India. So, if you stay in a building, it's worth checking out whether your building saves rainwater and how it does this. Typically, most buildings collect rainwater on their roofs and send it underground for storage, through pipes.

Even water treatment and recycling are picking up. Some residential buildings even have their own plants for doing this. One remarkable example is offered by T-ZED Homes in Bengaluru. It's possibly the only residential project in the world that treats, recycles and reuses all its wastewater and hardly needs any water from outside.

There are many ways in which different parts of India are trying to battle the water crisis—we just need to popularize them everywhere.

A number of people have devoted their lives to water conservation. Here are a few. Can you find out about others? Would you like to be like them?

In 1985, **Rajendra Singh** picked up a spade and, along with a villager, Nathi Bhalai, began digging a *johad*—a type of rainwater storage tank—at Gopalpura village in Rajasthan. Today, he is well-known as the Waterman of India and is widely credited for reviving water conservation, and bringing many rivers back to life in Rajasthan.

RAJENDRA SINGH

Agriculture consumes more than 80% of India's freshwater. But large amounts of it are wasted because of inefficient

AYYAPPA MASAGI

irrigation. Born into a family of farmers in Karnataka, **Ayyappa Masagi** studied mechanical engineering and worked for more than twenty years before returning to farming. He had purchased a few acres of land and decided to use this land as a laboratory to test and discover various solutions for water problems in agriculture. Today, he has helped thousands of water conservation projects across eleven states of India and is popularly called Water Gandhi, Water Magician and Water Doctor.

Aabid Surti is more than 80 years old. But age hasn't dented his will to fight India's water crisis—one leak at a time! He runs the Drop Dead Foundation, supported by one volunteer and one plumber, that takes care of small plumbing problems in Mumbai free-of-charge and saves water that would otherwise be wasted because of leaks.

AABID SURTI

16

Smokin' Delhi

Every year, as winter sets in Delhi, 9-year-old Janaki develops a phlegmy cough. Sometimes, she also gets fever. While the doctor prescribes medicines, he admits that Janaki's cough may continue to trouble her till the 'air clears up'. Janaki already knows. It's been happening to her for a few years. She's not sure when it started, but her mother says that even as a baby, Janaki used to fall sick in the winters. Two years ago, her parents got very worried—it had been nearly two months and Janaki's cough hadn't gone away. A continuous cough can be a symptom of many serious illnesses. Now they know, it's most probably the air, but they're still worried. Subhadra, who is 60 years old, has the same problem. She's lived in Delhi much longer than Janaki, but says that the coughing was never this bad . . .

What's happening to Janaki and Subhadra is not unusual for crores of people who live in Delhi. The air over the national capital and areas around it, like Gurugram and Noida, is often so polluted that it's compared to smoking anywhere between ten and fifty cigarettes.

Watch What You're Breathing

We say we breathe in oxygen. But actually, we breathe in air, which is a mixture of various gases. It is largely made up of nitrogen and oxygen, but it also has small amounts of other gases like carbon dioxide, argon and methane. Air is said to be polluted when anything changes this basic composition and makes air harmful for the environment. During the 1990s, scientists uncovered the health risks of one of the biggest villains in air pollution—aerosols.

The air you breathe today has lakhs of tiny solid particles and liquid droplets, such as dust, microbes, spores from plants and water. These particles suspended in air are called aerosols. You might have heard of them as PM 2.5 and PM 10. PM means Particulate Matter, while the numbers represent their size in microns. Both of these particles are several times smaller than a human hair. That's why it's easy for us to breathe them in. Once these particles, especially the solid ones, enter our body, they slowly start destroying our health and are a big cause of problems related to our heart and lungs. Janaki or Subhadra's cough might just have to do with an accumulation of these particles inside their bodies . . . But why in winter?

Pollutants are present in the air all the time, but they usually disperse when it's windy or settle down when it rains. However, during the winter, it hardly rains and the air is still, trapping pollutants in one place. Foggy air that's heavy with particulate matter is called smog. Every time you breathe during a smog, you take in more particulate matter because it's not getting dispersed or watered down!

While gases like carbon dioxide trap heat and make the planet warmer, aerosols reflect heat away from the planet and actually have a cooling effect. In fact, during the 1970s, some people were worried about global cooling because of aerosols.

Indian cities are some of the most polluted in the world. Delhi—the national capital—and areas surrounding it, which make up the National Capital Region (NCR), almost always top global air pollution rankings. Here are ten Indian cities that top the charts in air pollution.

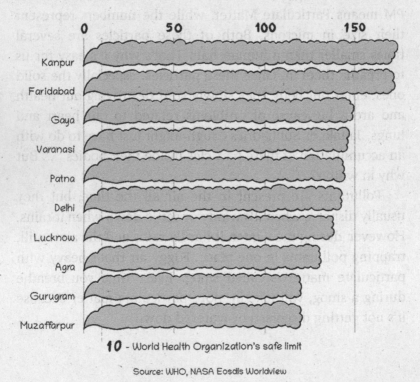

10 - World Health Organization's safe limit

Source: WHO, NASA Eosdis Worldview

The problem of air pollution in Delhi and NCR is quite old. Even during the 1990s, the region was often coated in black smog. But people didn't know enough about air pollution. However, organizations like the Centre for Science and Environment sensed danger and swung into action. Slowly, Delhi began its battle with dirty air.

Monitoring the Air

Today, all you need is a click of a button to find out how good or bad the air you're breathing is. This happens because air quality is closely monitored. But up until 1998, things were quite different. A law against air pollution had been passed in 1981, Pollution Control Boards had been set up and India even had a National Air Quality Monitoring Programme, yet nothing much was being done in the name of monitoring. In the aftermath of the visibly dirty air of the 1990s, the Environmental Pollution (Prevention and Control) Authority (EPCA) was set up in 1998 to tackle air pollution. Delhi began to set up a network of monitoring stations. Today, there are more than 600 such stations covering more than 250 cities across the country.

In 2015, we went one step further and launched the Air Quality Index (AQI) in India for reporting the air quality in more than 150 cities, including Delhi. AQI is what you'll most likely get, if you visit a website or download an app to know the quality of air in your city.

What does it mean if the AQI in your city is 159? Find out, using the index:

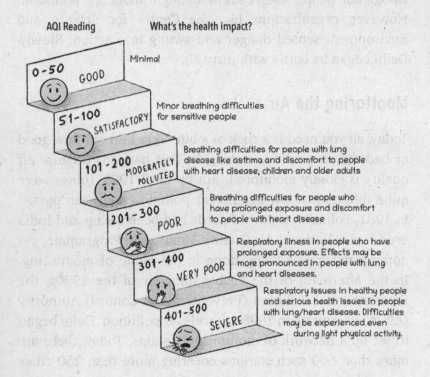

AQI Reading What's the health impact?

0-50 GOOD — Minimal

51-100 SATISFACTORY — Minor breathing difficulties for sensitive people

101-200 MODERATELY POLLUTED — Breathing difficulties for people with lung disease like asthma and discomfort to people with heart disease, children and older adults

201-300 POOR — Breathing difficulties for people who have prolonged exposure and discomfort to people with heart disease

301-400 VERY POOR — Respiratory illness in people who have prolonged exposure. Effects may be more pronounced in people with lung and heart diseases.

401-500 SEVERE — Respiratory issues in healthy people and serious health issues in people with lung/heart disease. Difficulties may be experienced even during light physical activity.

Monitoring and reporting air quality has been one of our biggest successes in the fight against air pollution. However, it has also given us reasons to worry. Delhi's AQI usually ranges between 'Poor' and 'Severe' and sometimes it breaches the index with readings of more than 500, which falls under the undocumented 'Severe Plus' category.

Polluted air is hazardous for our health. In fact, a 2019 study called 'State of Global Air' said 12 lakh people in India died because of air pollution in 2017.

So, what's making the air quality so bad? Some of the biggest polluters in Delhi are motor vehicles, industries and straw burning by farmers in neighbouring states.

The Cars We Drive

In newly independent India, owning a car was a luxury only the super-rich could afford. But in the 1980s, our automobile industry took off in a big way with the arrival of the relatively cheap Maruti 800. Suddenly, more and more people found they could afford the comfort and convenience of having their own car. The number of cars on the road began to increase.

The first Maruti 800 was given to Harpal Singh from Delhi. He had won it in a lucky draw.

A few years after Independence . . .

Today . . .

However, there was one big problem—both the technology as well as the fuel used in these cars polluted the environment by emitting a large amount of particulate matter and toxic gases like sulphur dioxide.

In 1999, India took its first major steps to clean up automobiles. Till then it did have some regulations around vehicle emissions, but in 2000 it adopted European emission and fuel regulations that began to be strictly applied on various four-wheeled vehicles. These are called the Bharat Stage (BS) emission standards and they are constantly being upgraded so vehicles have slowly been getting cleaner and cleaner.

But, the number of cars on our roads has not really come down. Delhi alone had more than 32 lakh cars and jeeps in 2018. The huge number of cars on its roads has meant that transport is responsible for more than a third of Delhi's air pollution during winter.

On 22 October 2015, Delhi marked its first car-free day. It was the third time that such an initiative was taken up in India to combat traffic and air pollution. Before Delhi, such initiatives had happened in Hyderabad and Gurugram.

Diesel Dilemma

Diesel is one of the more polluting fuels. Till the 1990s, it was primarily used in public transport such as buses and autos. Cars usually ran on petrol. But by the end of the decade something really strange happened in Delhi. Public transport began to switch over to using the much cleaner Compressed Natural Gas (CNG), while diesel cars were introduced on the roads. Delhi bid goodbye to its last diesel bus in 2002, but more and more buyers were tempted by diesel cars because diesel has always been relatively cheaper than petrol.

Nevertheless, strict emission standards and fuel regulations have ensured that diesel and four-wheelers running on it have become cleaner. For example, back in the 1990s, diesel had a large amount of sulphur, which released huge quantities of sulphur dioxide into the air when burnt. Regulations reduced the acceptable amount of sulphur in diesel from 0.5% to 0.05%, making it relatively cleaner and reducing sulphur dioxide emissions.

More recently, the government has been actively supporting electric cars that run on battery and do not produce emissions like cars running on diesel, petrol or even CNG. In fact, 2020 has been a breakthrough year for such cars because of the large number of new models introduced by different car makers. However, a lot remains to be seen about the future of such cars in India.

Let's Make Transport Public

On 24 December 2002, Prime Minister Atal Bihari Vajpayee bought a smart card and boarded the first Delhi Metro train at Kashmere Gate, alighting at Seelampuri. It may have been a short celebratory ride for the PM, but it was a giant leap for public transport in Delhi. Today, the metro has more than 270 stations spread across Delhi-NCR and transports over 25 lakh people every day. It has significantly increased the reach of public transport in the region that was mainly served by buses and autos in the past.

In 2011, the Delhi Metro Rail Corporation was also honoured by the United Nations for reducing greenhouse gas emissions. It saves about 6,30,000 tonnes of carbon from being emitted into the air every year.

The Metro has been the biggest success story of Delhi's public transport history. Many other cities in India, like Jaipur and Mumbai, have also been inspired to set up a similar system. But, we are yet to meet the ultimate aim of public transport—significantly reducing the number of cars on the road. One of the problems experts point out is 'last mile connectivity'. Simply put, it's still far easier to take a car from one place to another instead of using public transport which may not connect you directly to your destination and for which you may need to walk on dirty roads and jostle traffic.

Out on the Roads

Ever been stuck in traffic where your vehicle keeps jamming to a halt every few minutes? Not only is this most annoying, it also consumes more fuel, wears out a vehicle's engine and increases the amount of particulate matter emitted. One of the ways in which Delhi has tried to reduce traffic and fight air pollution is by adding more roads and flyovers and making them wider. Bypass roads, like the various expressways surrounding the city, have also been built to prevent vehicles going to other states from crossing the city. In the early 1970s, Delhi had roads that stretched a little over 8300 kilometres. But by 2001, this had expanded to more than 28,000 kilometres. However, road construction is also a source of air pollution.

The time clocks that you might find on some traffic lights in India were introduced in a bid to encourage drivers to stop their cars during a red light and save fuel.

Industrial Pollution

In the 1960s, Delhi was visualized as a no-pollution zone. But as the city developed, the number of industries increased and industrial emissions became one of the major causes of air pollution. In 1985, the issue of air pollution was brought before the Supreme Court and some of the first moves to curb industrial pollution came during the 1990s. The court ordered several small and large industrial units in Delhi to close down, while others were told to relocate from within the city to its borders. Industrial zones were earmarked and many restrictions were imposed on industries to measure and control emissions, including the banning of polluting industrial fuels like furnace oil and pet coke. In 2018, industries were ordered to start using Piped Natural Gas (PNG) as fuel.

Apart from industries, coal-burning thermal power plants have also been a source of air pollution. Since 2010, Delhi has slowly been shutting down these plants and replacing them with cleaner ones generating electricity from natural gas and renewable sources. In October 2018, it shut down the last of these, in Badarpur.

Grappling with Pollution

In the winter of 2016, the city activated an alert system to cope with air pollution. This was called the Graded Response Action Plan (GRAP) and included a series of emergency measures such as taking cars off the road and shutting down polluting power plants and construction activities to control air pollution.

No Firecrackers

In September 2015, parents of the toddlers Arjun Gopal, Aarav Bhandari and Zoya Bhasin, petitioned the Supreme Court, asking it to stop the use of firecrackers during festivals like Dussehra and Diwali. They claimed that children are the worst-affected by heavily-polluted air, especially during festivals,  because their lungs are not fully developed and they can easily fall victim to breathing difficulties and illnesses such as bronchitis.

A few years later, in 2018, the court ordered a full-fledged ban on regular firecrackers and urged citizens to buy green firecrackers that are 30% less polluting. The court also ordered various other restrictions on the sale and burning of firecrackers. Unfortunately, this hasn't stopped people from selling and buying them illegally. What this means is that the air quality continues to become especially bad after Diwali and several people get arrested.

Straw Burning

Every year, before the onset of the monsoon, farmers in the neighbouring states of Delhi, like Punjab and Haryana, get ready to plant paddy. Paddy is a water-hungry crop and if it's planted in the fields much before the monsoon, it uses up falling reserves of precious groundwater. So, in 2009, the states ordered farmers to begin planting paddy in their fields closer to the monsoon to stop groundwater depletion. But many claim that this move to conserve groundwater has ended up becoming one of the biggest reasons behind air pollution in Delhi.

When the farmers delayed the planting of paddy in their fields, they also had to delay the harvest. This meant that they had very little time to clear the straw left behind in their fields after harvesting. Winter was close and they had to prepare their fields for growing wheat.
The straw would come in the way of the sowing machines they used. That's why more and more farmers started setting the straw on fire. It was the easiest and cheapest option to get rid of it on time. Even though it reduced soil quality, fertilizers could help with this. That's how straw burning has become increasingly common at the onset of winter.

Given Delhi's geography—it's surrounded by land on all sides and no sea to dilute its emissions—it becomes especially vulnerable to what is happening in the land surrounding it. If industries and thermal power plants in Haryana release toxic fumes, they come to Delhi. If farmers burn straw the fumes come to Delhi. If it snows heavily in the hilly regions around it, a chill descends—making the winter worse than ever. Until efforts to limit the man-made reasons for air pollution don't succeed, the wind and the rain are Delhi's only respite from the pollutants clogging its air.

Not Just a City

Air pollution, especially in cities around the world, has a long history. Many of them from Donora in the US to London in the UK have suffered frightening bouts of black air during the 1940s and 50s. These cities emerged from the crises to become the clean cities of today because of a strict enforcement of laws against air pollution and rising environmental consciousness. Today, Indian cities, especially in the Gangetic plains of the north, are fighting a similar battle. Lots of steps have been taken to control air pollution since the 1990s and widespread media coverage of the crisis, especially since 2017, has meant that everyone—from the richest to the poorest—is aware of it. It remains to be seen how effectively we're able to implement the laws and use rising environmental consciousness to clear our skies and emerge from the blackness.

17

Powering the Future

It may be difficult for many of us to imagine life without electricity today. How else will we power the dizzying array of electronics—from mobile phones and computers to refrigerators, televisions, fans and lights—surrounding us? However, things were very different back in 1947 when most of the country did not have any electricity.

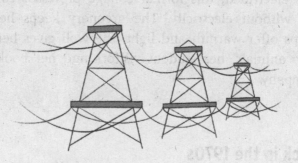

That's why, for a long time after Independence, India's focus was on generating and supplying as much electricity as possible to its citizens. No one really thought much about where this electricity was coming from. Thermal power stations burnt up fossil fuels like coal and oil to produce a bulk of our electricity.

The Woman Who Doesn't Need Electricity

In the middle of a busy street in Pune is an old, broken-down cottage, with a garden full of trees and an ancient well. It is home to a dog, two cats, a mongoose, a number of birds and an old lady named Hema Sane, who doesn't need electricity!

HEMA SANE

Hema was born nearly a decade before India became Independent. For her, electricity has always been something she could live without. After all, people were managing when they didn't have it. So, even today, when the world around her has electrified, this former college professor continues to live without electricity. The greenery keeps her cool, oil lamps offer warmth and light, the well gives her water and the animals, her student visitors and her books keep her company.

A Shock in the 1970s

For a long time, the world, including India, depended on large amounts of oil, apart from other fossil fuels, to produce electricity and run vehicles. Since a lot of the world's oil is found in the Middle East, most countries imported it from there. But during the 1970s, problems in the Middle East plunged the world into a crisis because countries were not able to procure enough oil! This made them realize that they had to find other sources of energy to power their growth.

This was how India, like a lot of other countries, first started looking more seriously at renewable sources of energy as well as energy efficiency. It was a slow beginning because we were a new country and had a lot to learn and do.

Renewable energy is produced by sources that nature has an endless supply of, such as wind, sunlight and water. Unlike fossil fuels such as coal and oil, these sources won't run out. Producing energy from renewable sources does not release large amounts of greenhouse gases, so it's environment-friendly too. However, we do not produce all our electricity from such sources because their supply is unsteady. For example, the sun doesn't shine at night or even at the same intensity throughout the day, while the wind may blow in different directions or not at all.

Hydropower

Damming rivers to generate hydroelectricity had been done in India much before Independence. The first hydropower projects were built by the British towards the end of the 19th century. Even after Independence, India continued damming its rivers to irrigate its fields and produce hydroelectricity.

Even though water is a renewable source of electricity, you might find that hydropower is often not included with other renewable sources of energy. This is usually because of the negative impact of dams on the natural environment and people living close to rivers.

Biogas

At the time of Independence, India was largely a rural country and agriculture dominated large parts of the land. So, it won't surprise you to know that one of our first sources of renewable energy was gas obtained from decomposing organic matter such as cattle dung and crop residue. This is also called biogas and it's mainly a mixture of methane and carbon dioxide.

Even our poop can be used to produce biogas. In fact, under a scheme in 2013, some villages in Gujarat linked their toilets to biogas plants.

A biogas plant is primarily used for producing cooking fuel and organic fertilizers. India's first biogas plants were set up by the Khadi and Village Industries Commission (KVIC) during the 1950s. The KVIC introduced the idea to farmers and their design continues to be used in many parts of India even today. Other models of biogas plants have also been introduced since the 1970s. During the 1980s, India started the National Biogas and Manure Management programme to promote biogas more widely in rural areas of the country.

Biogas plant with a farmer putting organic waste into it

Organic waste is put into a tank. As it decomposes, it produces biogas that is released through a pipe and used for cooking. It also forms sludge, which is a great organic fertilizer for plants.

Wind

The power of the wind has been used to do everything from sailing ships to grinding corn and pumping water. Independent India started experimenting with wind energy in a small way during the 1960s, to supply water for irrigation. It was only in the 1980s that wind power emerged as a source of electricity in India and the first wind power plants came up in Gujarat and Tamil Nadu. By the end of the decade, India had found its first significant renewable source of electricity. In 1998, it established the National Institute of Wind Energy (also called the Centre for Wind Energy Technology) in Chennai to research on and develop wind power in India. Today, India has some of the largest wind farms in the world. Among the biggest of these is at Jaisalmer in Rajasthan.

Windmills are mighty structures, but they generate electricity in quite a simple way—by having the wind rotate their fans!

Solar

While electricity for all has been one of India's major goals since Independence, taking regular electric transmission and distribution everywhere has always been a challenge. Most places in India get about 250 to 300 days of sunshine in a year. What if villages, especially in remote areas, could get electricity directly from the sun? During the 1990s, India started experimenting with this idea and by 2007, the first villages were taken up for electrification using solar power. Several Non-Governmental Organizations also joined the effort.

Solar lamps soon replaced old-fashioned kerosene lamps that caused air pollution and often led to fires. By 2009, more than six lakh such lamps had been distributed across villages.

Solar lamp

The success of early initiatives inspired India to ambitiously promote the use of solar energy and in 2010, it launched its National Solar Mission.

A few years later, in 2014, India announced that by 2022, it wanted to have the capacity to generate 100 gigawatts (GW) of solar energy. Suddenly, the entire world was listening to our solar story. Why? Because that's an incredible target. Even Germany—a global leader in solar energy—aims for a capacity of 66 GW by 2030!

Today, there's no stopping India's solar dreams. From solar-powered villages like Dharnai in Bihar to some of the biggest solar power projects in the world like Kamuthi in Tamil Nadu—India's attempts at harnessing the sun are rewriting its renewable energy history.

Solar panel on rooftop

Energy Efficiency

The next time you go to buy an electric appliance, visit a factory or even a building, inquire about its energy efficiency. Energy efficiency means using energy wisely, so you save more of it. Heard of the energy or power-saving mode on a mobile or laptop, for example? What it means is that your gadget will run using less than the usual amount of energy it uses.

In 2001 and 2003, India passed two laws—The Energy Conservation Act and The Electricity Act—that have led to major improvements in the way energy is used. Everything from the generation to the transmission and consumption of electricity has become more efficient.

The use of electricity has increased rapidly, especially in Indian households, as electronic appliances have become common. Some of these appliances, like refrigerators and air conditioners, use large amounts of electricity. Laws on energy efficiency have popularized the star-rating that you might find on these appliances today—more the number of stars, more the saving. So, if you have a four-star fridge, it uses less energy and automatically reduces your electricity bill.

Buildings use up a large amount of energy—mostly for lighting and cooling. During the 1990s, the US set up Leadership in Energy and Environmental Design (LEED), an initiative to promote energy-efficient, environmentally-sustainable buildings. Among other things, it popularized a rating system for buildings based on how 'green' they are. After the introduction of the energy efficiency laws, such ratings have become popular in India. From residential towers to hotels and offices—many buildings in our country have impressive green ratings today.

The CII-Sohrabji Godrej Green Business Centre in Hyderabad was one of the first buildings outside the US to get a LEED rating. It was constructed using a large amount of recycled material, such as broken glass and tiles and fly-ash and nearly all of the construction waste was also recycled. The building uses rainwater harvesting and also recycles all its waste water. Air-cooling towers sprinkle the air with water to cool it and gardens on the roof also bring down the temperature. This reduces the amount of air conditioning required. The building is designed in such a way that for a large part of the day it gets direct sunlight and doesn't need artificial lighting. These are among the many ways in which the building saves energy.

Many major industries in India from cement to iron and steel have also taken steps to become more energy-efficient and bring down their electricity bills, among other things.

Electrifying India

In 2018, after a tiny village in Manipur was connected to India's national electric grid, the government announced that every single village in the country had been electrified. It was called a historic event. After all, at the time of Independence, none of India's villages had any electricity.

> An electric grid is a network of cables that carry electricity from the producer and supply it to consumers.

While it is true that our national electric grid today is better connected than it ever was in history, many homes still remain in the dark. This is because transmission hasn't caught up with the production of electricity in our country and large amounts continue to be lost before they reach consumers. A constant, uninterrupted supply of electricity is still a long way off. That's why many buildings instal generators, that work like mini power stations, for backup.

Even though we continue getting a bulk of our electricity from burning fossil fuels, our capacity to generate it from renewable sources is increasing by the day. India is ambitiously marching towards a future where its development is powered by electricity drawn from the sun and the wind. It would be an astonishing feat if we succeed—and the world is watching closely.

Blackout!

In July 2012, India suffered one of its worst power cuts in history. Lakhs of people spread across twenty-one states were plunged into darkness because of a large-scale collapse in the national electric grid.

18

Waste in Space

The Earth may be drowning in waste (*see page 117*) but do you know what you're likely to find first if you blast off into space? A vast mass of floating space debris. While inactive satellites and broken pieces of satellites make up a bulk of it, increasing human presence in space has also left its mark. So, you might spot everything from tools like screwdrivers and pliers to gloves, cameras, garbage bags and even an astronaut's blanket!

How did so much waste get into space? Let's rewind to the dawn of the Space Age.

Poop and Pee in Space

Do you know the most uncomfortable part about being an astronaut? Relieving yourself in space. Alan Shepard, the first American in space, even peed in his pants because his spacecraft didn't have anything in the name of a toilet! Of course, it's become much better today. Astronauts are given equipment that catches and collects their waste, and they are even toilet trained. However, some of their fecal matter has added to space debris.

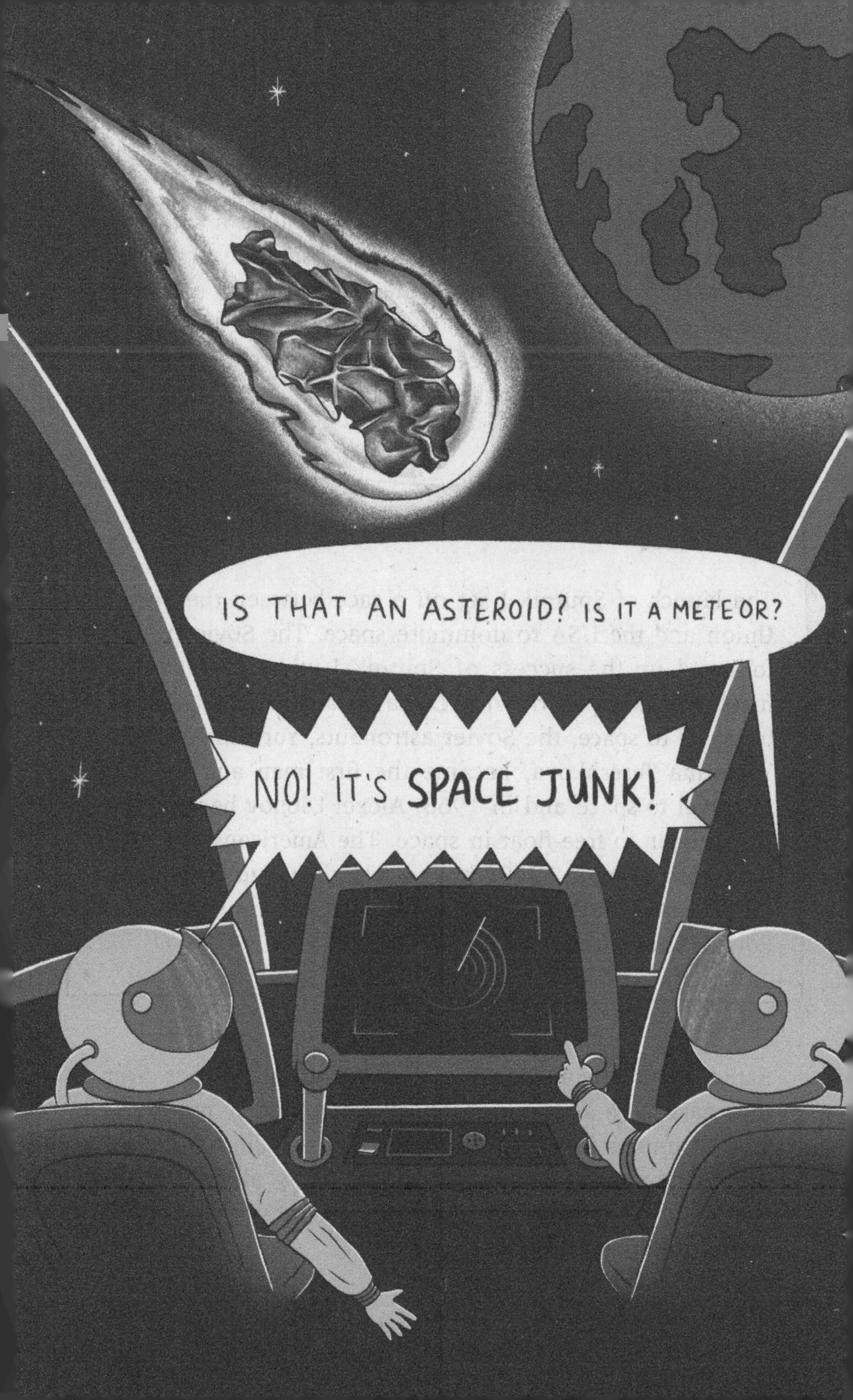
IS THAT AN ASTEROID? IS IT A METEOR?
NO! IT'S SPACE JUNK!

Satellites Galore

Any object that orbits another object is called a satellite. For example, the moon is the natural satellite of Earth. But in 1957, Russia (formerly the Soviet Union) officially kicked off the Space Age by launching Sputnik I, the first man-made satellite in space. Radio transmitters inside the satellite made a beeping sound that was heard all over the world.

Space Race

The launch of Sputnik I set off a race between the Soviet Union and the USA to dominate space. The Soviet Union followed up the success of Sputnik I with several other firsts. For example, the dog Laika became the first animal to travel to space, the Soviet astronauts, Yuri Gagarin and Valentina Tereshkova, became the first man and woman to travel to space and in 1965, Alexei Leonov became the first human to free-float in space. The Americans followed them closely but in 1969, they took 'a giant leap' by landing the first men on the moon—astronauts Neil Armstrong and Edwin 'Buzz' Aldrin.

Rapid advancement in space exploration meant that over the years more and more satellites were sent by more and more countries into Earth's orbit. These satellites stretched the boundaries of human knowledge. They allowed us to watch our planet like never before and transmitted signals seamlessly, from one place to another.

Satellites in Our Lives

From the Global Positioning System (GPS) used commonly in transportation to international telephone communication, TV dishes beaming different channels and weather forecasting—there are many services today that involve satellites.

Mounting Space Debris

Once a satellite enters space around the Earth, it begins to orbit our planet, sending signals carrying different information to space agencies on Earth. Eventually, gravity pulls it back into the Earth's atmosphere. Left to gravity alone, satellites would plunge right back to Earth. But the atmosphere makes it difficult for them to reach the planet and they usually burn up before they can hit the Earth's surface. For example, Sputnik I orbited Earth for three months before it re-entered the Earth's atmosphere and burnt up.

Fallen debris

Even though satellites burn up when they re-enter Earth's atmosphere, some pieces—a few hundred each year—do end up falling on Earth, usually inside waterbodies. Although there have been no reports of people being struck by falling space debris, if you do find a piece of such debris, don't try and touch it. It may be sizzling hot! A better idea would be to inform your space agency.

However, the farther a satellite moves from the Earth, the harder it becomes for gravity to pull it back. So, it continues to orbit our planet long after it stops sending signals and becomes inactive. A majority of satellites that orbit the Earth today are inactive. Having a large number of inactive satellites in orbit not only increases debris, it also increases the danger of collisions that end up generating even more debris. For example, in 2009, the active American satellite Iridium 33 collided with the inactive Russian satellite Cosmos 2251. This was the first collision between satellites and generated nearly 2000 pieces of debris, much of which is still orbiting Earth.

The oldest satellite still orbiting the Earth is Vanguard 1 which was launched by the USA in 1958 and became inactive in 1964.

Having so many satellites constantly surveying the Earth also carries a threat—what if, during a war, an enemy nation's satellite picks up secret military information? To counter this threat, countries also developed anti-satellite systems that can destroy enemy satellites. Destroying a satellite orbiting the Earth is like targeting a fast-moving object with a moving weapon—an impressive military feat. But, it's also a large source of space debris. For example, in 2007, when China destroyed one of its inactive satellites to test its anti-satellite system, it unleashed more than 3000 pieces of space debris.

In 2019, India grabbed international headlines for generating about 400 pieces of space debris. How did we do this? Let's uncover the fascinating story of our journey into space.

India in Space

During the 1950s, when space exploration began, newly independent India was struggling with too many problems to think of investing in a space programme of its own. But one powerful man, the industrialist-scientist Vikram Sarabhai, dreamt of seeing India in space. So, he convinced the government to set up the Indian National Committee for Space Research (INCOSPAR) in 1962. That's why Sarabhai is also called the Father of India's Space Programme.

Vikram Sarabhai

A year later, India began its space odyssey by launching a rocket from Thumba, a small fishing village in Kerala. A local church became the main office for the scientists, while the house and cattle-shed of the bishop served as their workshop and laboratory. When the rocket was ready, it was transported to the launch site on a bicycle!

In 1969, INCOSPAR grew into the Indian Space Research Organisation (ISRO). From sending India's first satellite Aryabhata into space in 1975 to setting a world record by launching 104 satellites together in one rocket in 2017, ISRO has achieved several milestones in space exploration within a few decades. In 2019, it helped India become the fourth nation in the world after Russia, the USA and China to successfully

Transporting a rocket on a bicycle at Thumba

test an anti-satellite system. Shortly after the test, National Aeronautics and Space Administration (NASA) pointed out that it had identified about 400 pieces of space debris created by the test. It was the first time that India's contribution to space waste made headlines around the world. In its defence, India said the explosion was relatively close to Earth and all the debris is likely to be pulled in by gravity and burnt up.

Dealing with Debris

During the 1960s, international space laws were created by the UN Committee on Peaceful Uses of Outer Space. Among other things, they tried to limit space debris. For example, by asking countries to develop satellites that didn't remain in orbit indefinitely and imposing penalties on countries whose spacecraft generated debris. However, a lot of these laws are not mandatory and many countries don't follow them.

Several countries track debris to avoid collisions and prevent more debris from being generated. Among the most notable is the US Space Surveillance Network that has been monitoring different objects in space since the beginning of the Space Age. ISRO too is currently working on building a facility to do this. But very tiny pieces are hard to track.

Efforts are also being made to find ways of clearing space debris. Proposals include grabbing debris using robotic arms and throwing giant nets over it. But this is easier said than done. Space is overcrowded and ensuring that a clean-up only targets debris and not active satellites can be difficult. If a clean-up accidentally targets a satellite containing sensitive information, it could be seen as an act of aggression and lead to war. Clearly, humans have generated a massive waste problem even in space!

Alice Gorman from Australia, also known as Dr Space Junk, is a pioneer in the field of Space Archaeology. For her, not all space debris is garbage. Some of it is a valuable piece of human history in space and needs to be preserved—unless it's posing a big risk.

19

Climate Catastrophe

A lot of people might tell you that climate change is nothing new. It's true. The Earth's climate has been changing throughout its history, which goes back billions of years. Sometimes it's been extremely hot and sometimes it's been extremely cold. However, in the past, climate change was driven by natural reasons. Today, a lot of it is happening because human activities like burning fossil fuels and cutting down forests are filling up the atmosphere with gases like carbon dioxide. Much like a greenhouse, these gases trap the sun's heat to keep the Earth warm. That's why they're known as greenhouse gases (GHGs).

The Earth has a natural ability to control the level of GHGs in its atmosphere by sinking excess amounts in forests and oceans. However, the industrial revolution in the 18th century began to destroy this ability. Mass burning of fossil fuels started generating large amounts of GHGs, while mass felling of forests to obtain industrial raw materials started damaging the natural sinks. The percentage of GHGs in our atmosphere started increasing beyond acceptable levels. Today, there is about 0.04% of carbon dioxide in our atmosphere. Climatologist James Hansen says that it shouldn't have crossed 0.03%.

There are many types of GHGs, such as methane and nitrous oxide. However, carbon dioxide gets a lot more attention. This is because it's found in a higher quantity and hangs around in the air for many more years than most others.

The increasing amounts of GHGs is making many places unusually warm—this is called global warming and it's got everyone worried. Beyond a certain temperature, our planet will no longer be able to support existing life and there may be yet another mass extinction.

Mass extinctions are deadly events driven by extreme changes in the Earth's climate that have wiped out entire species. Dinosaurs are a prime example of this. In the last 50 crore years, life on Earth has suffered a handful of these catastrophes. However, each mass extinction has also been followed by the blooming of new life forms suited to the changed climate.

Climate Change in the Headlines

In 1896, the Swedish scientist Svante Arrhenius became the first person to predict how burning fossil fuels like coal could cause global warming. But Arrhenius didn't see this as a bad thing. He thought it might bring some warmth to colder regions!

It was only in the 1980s that the world really began to worry about climate change. Temperatures had soared unusually. Many parts of the world were struck by acute heatwaves and drought. Fires broke out in the Amazon rainforest. The Intergovernmental Panel on Climate Change (IPCC) was established in 1988. It is a dedicated body of scientists that studies human-induced climate change, its impact on the planet and how to address it.

A few years later, in 1992, more than 100 countries, including India, came together for the first Earth Summit at Rio De Janeiro. There, they discussed ways to tackle the climate crisis and signed an international environmental treaty—the United Nations Framework Convention on Climate Change (UNFCCC). Participating in the summit and signing the UNFCCC was an important milestone in India's battle against the changing climate.

Climate Crisis in India

At the beginning of 2020, the Indian Meteorological Department (IMD) revealed that the previous decade had been the hottest since records began in 1901. However, India has been grappling with rising temperatures since the 1950s. During the 1950s, places with a mean maximum temperature greater than 40 degrees Celsius were limited to just a small area. However, this area started expanding in the 1970s and accelerated significantly by the 2000s. Today, large parts of the country, especially in the northwest and southern regions, suffer from acute warming.

As temperatures soar, especially in the drier regions, there are intense heatwaves and droughts. Meanwhile, warm air keeps accumulating moisture, increasing episodes of unusually heavy rainfall and flooding, especially in wetter regions. Warming oceans also become a breeding ground for cyclones that batter coastal regions with strong winds and heavy rainfall.

All of these—heatwaves, droughts, floods and cyclones—are forms of extreme weather that has become increasingly common in India over the past few decades. Some of the most widely reported extreme weather events of the last decade include the 2013 flash floods in Uttarakhand, when the state received 847% more rainfall than usual; cyclonic storms such as Amphan, along the historically battered eastern coast and severe heatwaves that swept the nation in 2016 when the temperature soared 0.71 degrees Celsius above average and

Phalodi in Rajasthan reached a record-breaking 51 degrees Celsius. By following the news, you too can keep a diary of all the extreme weather that is reported in India every year . . .

If you go to a place and find that it's hot, you would say that the weather is hot. But, if it remains hot for long periods of time—at least thirty years—you would say that the climate is hot.

Melting Glaciers, Rising Seas

Glaciers in the Hindu Kush region of the Himalayas have been melting at an alarming rate because of global warming. The extra water that comes from melting glaciers flows into the rivers they feed, increasing the danger of floods. Eventually, these rivers flow into the sea, causing a rise in sea levels.

The Gangotri glacier in the Hindu Kush region that feeds the river Ganga, has receded by over 1.5 kilometres in the last 100 years and continues to recede at an average rate of more than 10 metres annually. The Ganga is India's longest river and it flows through some of the most densely populated areas in the country—home to over 40 crore people. The melting glacier has increased the danger of floods in these areas that already suffer from unseasonal and often heavy rainfall.

Over the past few decades, the sea level around India has been rising by about 1.3 mm each year. The rise has been the sharpest along Diamond Harbour in West Bengal. However, most of this rise is because the gigantic ice sheets in Antarctica and Greenland are melting and not because of the melting glaciers of the Hindu Kush region.

If the Greenland ice sheet melts completely, the sea level would rise by 6000 mm and if the Antarctic ice sheet melts completely, it would rise by 60,000 mm! As a country with a coastline of more than 7000 kilometres, this would change our land forever.

An Uncertain Future

In the face of extreme weather events and other disasters, especially the 2004 Indian Ocean tsunami, India passed the National Disaster Management Act in 2005 and set up the National Disaster Management Authority. Over the last few years, disaster management—especially the early warning system—has helped save many lives. For example, a record 12 lakh people were evacuated in less than forty-eight hours and taken to cyclone shelters before Cyclone Fani struck the state of Odisha unexpectedly in the summer of 2019. Nearly 7000 kitchens were made functional overnight to cater to the shelters and more than 45,000 volunteers were engaged. This was a far cry from 1999, when another severe cyclonic storm had battered Odisha and killed more than 10,000 people because of the lack of an early warning and disaster management system.

However, extreme weather, melting glaciers and rising sea level may just be the tip of the iceberg. From islands and forests to deserts, mountains and plateaus—India is one of the most geographically diverse countries on the planet, with an equally large and diverse population. So, it's hard to predict how exactly increasing temperatures will affect it. However, some problems have already started unfolding prominently. Here are a few, can you think of others?

Climate Migrants

Large numbers of people have been displaced by extreme weather that not just destroys their homes, but also their livelihoods. For example, several fishermen migrated to  other areas in search of work after cyclones struck Odisha. The Internal Displacement Monitoring Centre (IDMC) found that between 2008 and 2018, about 36 lakh people were displaced annually within India, primarily because of flooding during the rainy season. That's larger than the population of many small countries in the world!

Agricultural Distress

About 68% of India is prone to droughts yet more than 50% of farmland continues to rely on rainfall for irrigation. During the 1960s, back-to-back droughts set the stage for the Green Revolution in India (*see page 9*). Even  though food production has increased in India, climate change could have an adverse impact on widely-grown, water-guzzling crops like paddy. Farmers could end up losing up to 25% of their income due to lack of production and joining the growing number of climate migrants.

Health

Extreme weather often leads to an outbreak of water- and vector-borne diseases, such as dengue, malaria, cholera and diarrhoea. The weather also affects our mood, and research shows exposure to extreme weather may lead to excessive stress,  depression and anxiety. Moreover, rising temperatures not only trigger heat stress in the body, but may also cause a drop in the quantity and quality of food produced by agriculture, leading to malnutrition. The World Health Organization predicts that between 2030 and 2050 about 2,50,000 more people may die because of malaria, diarrhoea, heat stress and malnutrition.

Loss of Biodiversity

India is home to about 7–8% of all plant and animal species found on our planet. Many of them are endemic—they're only found in India. Plants and animals as well as their habitats are sensitive to climatic conditions such as

temperature and rainfall. Species that adapt continue to thrive but many are also becoming endangered.

Fighting Uncertainty

Following the Rio Summit, India has been mapping its carbon emissions and has undertaken increasingly detailed studies to assess the different ways in which climate change will affect its land and its people. In 2008 it also implemented a National Action Plan for Climate Change—eight missions that it hopes will help it in its fight against the changing climate.

20

National Action Plan for Climate Change

India is the second-most populated country in the world with a large number of poor people. It's already struggling with rising temperatures—the previous decade has broken all records to become the hottest till date. If global temperatures increase by more than a degree Celsius, we would be among the worst-affected.

According to the Global Climate Risk Index published by Germanwatch, India was the fifth most affected country in 2018. More than 320 people died and over 2,20,000 were displaced because of the floods in Kerala. About 20,000 houses and eighty dams were destroyed. Meanwhile, the cyclones Titli and Gaja battered the east coast. Although the early warning system saved many people from dying, around 4,50,000 people were left without electricity for a long time and many coastal communities lost their homes and livelihood.

Ever since the first Earth Summit in 1992, India has been an important participant in global meets on tackling the climate crisis. In 2008, it became one of the handful of countries around the world to announce a comprehensive plan to fight climate change. This was the National Action Plan for Climate Change (NAPCC) and it listed eight key missions India would undertake to mitigate risks and adapt to the changing climate.

National Solar Mission: Launched in 2010, for harnessing as much solar energy as possible for power generation and other uses.

National Mission for Enhanced Energy Efficiency: Launched in 2010, for encouraging large, energy-consuming industries such as aluminium, iron and steel, cement and paper to become energy-efficient.

National Mission on Sustainable Habitat: Launched in 2010, for promoting sustainable cities with energy-efficient buildings, effective waste management and recycling, vehicles that use fuel economically, energy-efficient vehicles like electric cars and a high-use of public transportation.

National Water Mission: Launched in 2011, for fighting water scarcity by increasing efficient use of water.

Green India Mission: Launched in 2014, for increasing India's green cover through afforestation of lakhs of hectares of land.

National Mission for Sustaining the Himalayan Ecosystem: Launched in 2010, for saving Himalayan glaciers from melting and protecting the region's biodiversity.

National Mission for Sustainable Agriculture: Launched in 2012, for helping agriculture cope with climate change through various means, like the development of climate-resilient crops.

National Mission on Strategic Knowledge for Climate Change: Launched in 2014, for gaining a better understanding of climate science and the impact and challenges of climate change in order to come up with ways to adapt and reduce problems.

The Tale of a Climate Scientist

As a young boy growing up in a farming community in Karnataka, N.H. Ravindranath was fascinated by his grandfather's ability to forecast the monsoon. 'Farmers used to visit him all the time and he would pull out the lunar calendar and tell them when they were to sow which crops based on expected rainfall. He used to be right most of the time.' Witnessing this scene made young Ravindranath realize the huge importance of the weather for agriculture. That's how he decided to become a climate scientist and study the impact of climate on the natural world and the human beings depending on it.

For a long time, he was one of the few climate scientists working at the famous Indian Institute of Science in Bengaluru. 'It was not until the 1990s that scientific analysis of the impact of climate change in different areas like agriculture, forestry, water and health began to gain importance in India. We were all very excited when India decided to work on the NAPCC.'

Unfortunately, the speed with which the climate is changing today is bewildering. Ravindranath minces no words when he says, 'India already has a lot of problems such as poor healthcare, unirrigated agriculture, soil erosion and contaminated and depleting groundwater. Climate change and environmental degradation would only make matters worse, especially for poor people who are already suffering because they don't have sufficient resources to protect themselves.

'Climate change is such a big problem that it would be impossible to fight it unless everyone takes action. Children too have a role to play. Today, many children are becoming climate activists by protesting against climate change. But what is even more effective is if they try and control their carbon footprint and actively encourage everyone, from their family to their friends to do this. This would mean taking small steps like not wasting water, thinking before buying and throwing away things and taking the school bus instead of going in a car.

'There's a lot to do and environmentally conscious and considerate children are perhaps the biggest security we can have for the future.'

Last Words

So far, India has found mixed success in its national missions under the NAPCC. However, during the 2014 climate conference in Paris, it surprised the world with its incredibly ambitious commitment to combat climate change.

Carbon emissions by different countries are the main reason behind climate change. Hence, from the very beginning, reducing emissions has been a key goal of global meets to address the changing climate. Initially, it was felt that developed countries that had been at the helm of the industrial revolution should take responsibility and cut their emissions. India agreed with this. After all, developing countries that started industrializing much later had to be given more room to grow. Forcing them to cut emissions might halt their economic growth and this would be unfair, given that they contribute a smaller percentage of global carbon emissions. For example, India only contributes about 6%. However, at the Paris conference, India agreed to cut its own emissions instead of insisting that developed countries cut theirs first and set three major goals to be achieved between 2020 and

2030. These are—to generate about 40% of its power from non-fossil fuels, to reduce the level of emissions by 33–35% of what they were in 2005 and to add enough forest and tree cover to absorb carbon emissions.

Will India meet this target? How will its fight against the changing climate affect its growth and what does it stand to gain and lose? The stage has been set for an epic combat and the story will continue to evolve through our lifetime.

The Years after Independence: A Timeline

1947—Independence and Partition of India

1954—The Bhabha Atomic Research Centre is established

1962—Indian National Committee for Space Research (INCOSPAR) is established

1963—Bhakra Dam, the first large dam being built in independent India, is completed

1965—Green Revolution is introduced

1969—India's first nuclear power plant is established; INCOSPAR becomes the Indian Space Research Organisation (ISRO)

1970—Operation Flood, a national milk revolution, is launched

1972—First environmental law after Independence, the Wildlife Protection Act is passed

1973—Project Tiger is launched; Chipko movement breaks out in Uttarakhand

1974—First nuclear bomb is tested; Central Pollution Control Board is established; Water (Prevention and Control of Pollution) Act is passed

1981—Air (Prevention and Control of Pollution) Act is passed

1983—Decision to build a dam in Silent Valley is called off

1984—Deadly gas leaks out of a pesticide factory in Bhopal, it's called the worst industrial disaster in the world

1985—Ministry of Environment, Forest and Climate Change (formerly Ministry of Environment and Forest) is established

1986—India passes the historic Environment Protection Act; Ganga Action Plan implemented to clean the Ganga

1989—Beej Bachao Andolan—Save the Seeds Movement—begins in Uttarakhand

1992—Project Elephant is launched; Ministry of New and Renewable Energy is (formerly Ministry of Non-Conventional Energy Sources) established; India becomes a party to the United Nations Framework Convention on Climate Change after the Earth Summit at Rio De Janeiro

1996—Supreme Court acts to save the Taj Mahal from pollution

1998—India declares itself a Nuclear-Weapons State after testing five bombs; Environmental Pollution (Prevention and Control) Authority is established

2000—Municipal Solid Waste (Management and Handling) rules are passed

2004—Indian Ocean tsunami batters the east coast

2005—National Disaster Management Act is passed

2008—India announces its National Action Plan for Climate Change (NAPCC)

2009—News breaks out about uranium poisoning in Punjab

2010—National Green Tribunal is established; National Solar Mission, National Mission for Enhanced Energy Efficiency, National Mission for Sustaining the Himalayan Ecosystem and National Mission on Sustainable Habitat are launched

2011—National Water Mission is launched

2012—Anti-nuclear energy protests at Kudankulam intensify after the Fukushima Disaster; biggest power cut in India following failure in the national electric grid; National Mission for Sustainable Agriculture is launched

2014—Swachh Bharat Abhiyan is launched; India makes an ambitious commitment to cut its carbon emissions at a climate conference near Paris; Green India Mission and National Mission on Strategic Knowledge for Climate Change are launched

2015—Air Quality Index (AQI) launched in India

2017—Despite decades of protests against it, the Sardar Sarovar Dam in the Narmada is inaugurated in Gujarat; Great Smog of Delhi hits national headlines

2018—Government declares that every village in India has been electrified

2019—Chennai runs out of water; lakhs of people evacuated and saved from Cyclone Fani in Odisha

2020—Indian Meteorological Department reveals that the last decade is the hottest on records; the coronavirus pandemic forces India to impose a historic lockdown

Acknowledgements

Christopher Hill, for encouraging me from the very beginning of this journey

Radhika Suri, the opportunities you gave me have inspired this book

Bittu Sahgal, Ramachandra Guha and Ridhima Pandey for the foreword, blurb and advance praise that add so much to this book

Carin Smit, Manash Chatterjee, M.C. Mehta, N. Ravindranath, Raman Sukumar, Sanjay Upadhyay, Vinod Rishi and Vivek Menon for your valuable help and inputs

Sohini Mitra, Smit Zaveri, Aditi Shastry, Shalini Agrawal, Devangana Dash, Tathagata Sen and Kafeel Ahmad at Penguin India, for helping to bring this book to life—may it be a long and fruitful one.

Radhika Menon, most of what I know about a good children's book is because of Tulika.

Mom, dad and *bhai* for always having my back. I'm here because of your relentless support and belief in me.

My friends, for being the best sounding boards.

Bibliography

A listing of main sources used for each chapter

Chapter 1: When You Divide a Land

1. Hill, Christopher. *South Asia: An Environmental History*. California: ABC-CLIO, 2008
2. Sanyal, Sanjeev. *The Incredible History of India's Geography*. Gurgaon: Penguin Books, 2015
3. Chatterji, Joya. *The Spoils of Partition: Bengal and India, 1947-1967*. New York: Cambridge University Press, 2007
4. Chattha, Ilyas. 'After the Massacres: Nursing Survivors of Partition Violence in Pakistan Punjab Camps' *Journal of the Royal Asiatic Society* 28, no. 2 (April 2018): 273-293, https://www.cambridge.org/core/journals/journal-of-the-royal-asiatic-society/article/after-the-massacres-nursing-survivors-of-partition-violence-in-pakistan-punjab-camps/A306445A415255571B5A739D5CB31A3B/core-reader
5. 'Treaty Between India And The Bangladesh On Sharing Of The Ganges Waters At Farakka' retrieved from https://iea.uoregon.edu/treaty-text/1996-sharinggangesentxt

6. Choudhury, Kamran Reza. 'The Ganga Treaty: Ainun Nishat on How India, Bangladesh Signed a Historic Deal' Accessed on March 28, 2020 https://www.firstpost.com/long-reads/the-ganga-treaty-ainun-nishat-on-how-india-bangladesh-signed-a-historic-deal-5208161.html
7. Interviews with family members of three partition survivors from Punjab in India

Chapter 2: 'Green' Revolution?

1. Hill, Christopher. *South Asia: An Environmental History*. California: ABC-CLIO, 2008
2. Nitya Rao. *MS Swaminathan in Conversation with Nitya Rao: A farmer-led approach to achieving a malnutrition-free India*. Chennai: M.S. Swaminathan Research Foundation, 2016
3. Kesavan, P.C. *M.S. Swaminathan: The Quest for a World Without Hunger*. Chennai: M.S. Swaminathan Research Foundation, 2017
4. Dalal, Roshen. *A History of India for Children*. Gurgaon: Penguin Books, 2003
5. Barwale, Badrinarayan. 'When the Green Revolution Came to India'. The Borlaug Blog. Published July 25, 2017. https://www.worldfoodprize.org/index.cfm/88533/18096/when_the_green_revolution_came_to_india
6. Academic Kids Encyclopedia. 'Norman Borlaug'. Accessed August 21, 2018. https://academickids.com/encyclopedia/index.php/Norman_Borlaug
7. Pingali, Prabhu L. 'Green Revolution: Impacts, limits, and the path ahead'. PNAS Proceedings of the National Academy of Sciences of the United States of America.

Published online July 31, 2012. https://www.ncbi.nlm.nih.gov/pmc/articles/PMC3411969/

8. Inputs from Manash Chatterjee

Chapter 3: Dammed!

1. Guha, Ramachandra. *India After Gandhi: A History of the World's Largest Democracy*. London: Pan Macmillan, 2007
2. Hill, Christopher. *South Asia: An Environmental History*. California: ABC-CLIO, 2008
3. 'Large Dams in India'. Accessed on November 2, 2018. http://scholar.harvard.edu/files/rpande/files/large_dams_in_india.pdf
4. Warrier, Gopikrishna S. 'Silent Valley: A controversy that focused global attention on a rainforest 40 years ago'. Published on February 1, 2018. *Mongabay: News and Inspiration from Nature's Frontline*
5. Dattatri, Shekar. 'Silent Valley – A People's Movement that Saved a Forest' Accessed on November 2, 2018. https://www.conservationindia.org/case-studies/silent-valley-a-peoples-movement-that-saved-a-forest
6. Lal, Pranay. *Indica: A Deep Natural History of the Indian Subcontinent*. Gurgaon: Penguin Random House India, 2016
7. Krishnan, Priya. *Read and Colour River Stories: The Story of Narmada*. Chennai: Tulika Publishers, 2002

Chapter 4: India's Milk Revolution

1. Chowdhury, Rohini. *Verghese Kurien: The Milkman of India*. Gurgaon: Scholastic India Pvt Ltd, 2014

2. National Dairy Development Board. 'Children's Corner'. Published in 2015. https://www.nddb.coop/ccnddb/milk-facts

3. 'Environmental/Ecological Impact of the Dairy Sector: Literature review on dairy products for an inventory of key issues List of environmental initiatives and influences on the dairy sector'. *Bulletin of the International Dairy Federation*, 436 (2009)

4. Press Trust of India, 'Mother Dairy to collect 1,000 kg waste plastic in Delhi-NCR by Oct 2'. Published on September 27, 2019 in *Business Standard*

5. Vitta, Shweta. 'Akshayakalpa Farms – how IT professionals are turning into farm-based entrepreneurs in Karnataka's Tiptur'. Published on February 16, 2016. https://yourstory.com/2016/02/akshayakalpa-farms

Chapter 5: Tiger Tales

1. Thapar, Valmik. *Tiger Fire: 500 years of the Tiger in India*. New Delhi: Aleph Book Company, 2013

2. Thapar, Valmik. *The Last Tiger: Struggling for Survival*. New Delhi: Oxford University Press, 2012

3. Edited by Rangarajan, Mahesh and Sivaramakrishnan, K. *India's Environmental History: Colonialism, Modernity and the Nation*. Ranikhet: Permanent Black, 2014

4. 'Tourism in Tiger Reserves'. *Sanctuary Magazine*. Vol XXXII No. 4 (August 2012)

5. Edited by Jhala, Y.V., Gopal, R. and Qureshi, Q. *Status of Tigers, co-predators and prey in India*. National Tiger Conservation Authority and Wildlife Institute of India, 2008

6. Edited by Taylor, V.J. and Dunstone, N. *The Exploitation of Mammal Populations*. London: Chapman & Hall, 1996

Bibliography

Chapter 6: The Price of a Forest

1. Hill, Christopher. *South Asia: An Environmental History*. California: ABC-CLIO, 2008
2. Gadgil, Madhav and Guha, Ramachandra. *This Fissured Land: An Ecological History of India*. New Delhi: Oxford University Press, 1992
3. Notification by the Government of Karnataka, accessed on September 23, 2019 https://aranya.gov.in/downloads/raising%20Of%20neelgiri.pdf
4. Sundararaju, V. 'How alien invasive plant species threaten Western Ghats' Published on November 28, 2018. https://www.downtoearth.org.in/blog/forests/how-alien-invasive-plant-species-threaten-western-ghats-62294
5. 'Coral tree (Erythrina variegata)'. Published on August 2, 2019. https://www.feedipedia.org/node/23080
6. Pandya, Mamata. *The Coral Tree*. Chennai: Tulika Publishers, 2011
7. Vachcharajani, Bijal. *So You Want to Know About the Environment*. New Delhi: Rupa Publications India Pvt Ltd. 2017
8. Joshi, Apoorva. 'One Man plants forest larger than Central Park' Published on November 13, 2014. *Mongabay: News and Inspiration from Nature's Frontline*
9. Swamy, Kumara V. 'Saalumarada Thimmakka: The Green Centenarian' Published on January 19, 2020 *Reader's Digest*
10. 'Shubhendu Sharma' Accessed on January 20, 2020 https://www.ashoka.org/en-in/fellow/shubhendu-sharma

Chapter 7: Is Nuclear Energy Bad?

1. Guha, Ramachandra. *India After Gandhi: A History of the World's Largest Democracy*. London: Pan Macmillan, 2007

199

2. U.S. Department of Energy. *The History of Nuclear Energy*. Accessed on February 7, 2018 https://www.energy.gov/sites/prod/files/The%20History%20of%20Nuclear%20Energy_0.pdf

3. 'India's Nuclear Weapons Programme: The Beginning 1944-1960'. Published March 30, 2001. https://nuclearweaponarchive.org/India/IndiaOrigin.html

4. Nuclear Threat Initiative. 'India'. Accessed on February 7, 2018. https://www.nti.org/learn/countries/india/nuclear/

5. Intercultural Resources, Kanti Bose, Tarun. 'Kudankulam Nuclear Power Plant: Nucleus of Disaster' Published on June 12, 2013. https://www.ritimo.org/Kudankulam-Nuclear-Power-Plant-Nucleus-of-Disaster

6. Joshi, Manoj. 'India is waking up from nuclear energy dream'. Published on April 1, 2019. https://www.orfonline.org/research/india-waking-nuclear-energy-dream-49434/

7. 'Reactor side problem, one unit at Kudankulam shut down'. Published on February 14, 2020. https://www.dtnext.in/News/Business/2020/02/14123050/1215154/Reactor-side-problem-one-unit-at-Kudankulam-shut-down.vpf

8. Auner, Eric. 'India passes Nuclear Liability Bill'. Accessed on February 1, 2020. https://www.armscontrol.org/act/2010-10/india-passes-nuclear-liability-bill

9. 'Non-Renewable Energy' Accessed on March 4, 2020 https://www.nationalgeographic.org/encyclopedia/non-renewable-energy/

Chapter 8: 'Seeds' of History

1. 'Saving the Seeds: Conserving India's agricultural biodiversity'. Accessed on September 10, 2018. http://

moef.gov.in/wp-content/uploads/wssd/doc3/chapter11/css/Chapter11.htm

2. Gifford, Dawn. 'The Difference Between Open Pollinated, Hybrid and GMO Seeds' Accessed on October 2, 2019. https://www.smallfootprintfamily.com/hybrid-seeds-vs-gmos

3. Ramesh, Mridula. *The Climate Solution: India's Climate Change Crisis and What We Can Do About It.* Gurgaon: Hachette Book Publishing India Pvt Ltd, 2018

4. Dobson, Jim. 'A Doomsday Vault In India Holds Frozen Storage For The Survival Of Future Generations'. Published on February 23, 2019. *Forbes*

5. Vachcharajani, Bijal. *The Seed Savers.* Pratham Books, 2018

6. Times News Network. 'Why India's native crops need to be saved from extinction' Published on January 17, 2020. https://timesofindia.indiatimes.com/why-indias-native-crops-need-to-be-saved-from-extinction/articleshow/73237886.cms

7. Inputs from Manash Chatterjee

Chapter 9: Nightmare in Bhopal

1. Mahapatra Richard, Yadav Archana, Bhushan Chandra, Varshney Vibha, Narain Sunita, Sharma Aruna, Gupta Kaushik. *Bhopal Gas Tragedy After 30 Years*, New Delhi: Centre for Science and Environment, 2014

2. Hill, Christopher. *South Asia: An Environmental History.* California: ABC-CLIO, 2008

Chapter 10: Gentle Giants

1. 'Asian Elephant'. Accessed on December 19, 2019 https://nationalzoo.si.edu/animals/asian-elephant

2. Govier, Jenna. 'Four Reasons Why the Environment Needs Elephants' Accessed on December 19, 2019 https://www.gvi.co.uk/blog/4-reasons-need-elephants/

3. Edited by Menon Vivek, Tiwari Sandeep KR, Ramkumar K, Kyarong Sunil, Ganguly Upasana and Sukumar Raman. *Right of Passage: Elephant Corridors of India*. New Delhi: Wildlife Trust of India, 2017

4. 'Glimpses of Initiatives Taken for Elephant Conservation in India (2012-2017) based on Parliamentary Questions and Replies'. ENVIS Centre, WWF India, Project Elephant Division, Ministry of Environment, Forests and Climate Change

5. Menon Vivek, Sukumar Raman and Kumar Ashok, *A God in Distress: Threats of Poaching and the Ivory Trade to the Asian Elephant in India*, New Delhi: Wildlife Protection Society of India, 1997

6. Baskaran N., Varma Surendra, Sar C. K. and Sukumar Raman. "Current Status of Asian Elephants in India" Asian Nature Conservation Foundation, 2011

7. 'Battle zone: Humans vs elephants'. Published on June 7, 2015. https://www.downtoearth.org.in/coverage/battle-zone-humans-vs-elephants-12661

8. Sukumar, Raman. 'Project Elephant: Answering a Distress Call' *The Hindu Survey of the Environment*, 1996

9. Sridharan Vasudev, 'How a Karnataka town used SMS alerts to reduce human-elephant conflicts' Published on March 14, 2019. https://scroll.in/article/915480/how-a-karnataka-town-used-sms-alerts-to-reduce-human-elephant-conflicts

10. Abraham, Mary-Rose. 'Can Bees Save Elephants from Train Strikes' Published on June 20, 2018, https://www.nationalgeographic.com/news/2018/06/reducing-

elephant-train-collisions-india-bee-buzzing-animals-environment/

11. '429 elephants killed since 2008, 642 poachers arrested' Published on January 10, 2019. *Press Trust of India*

12. Bist, S.S. 'An Overview of Elephant Conservation in India' *The Indian Forester* Vol 128, Issue 2 (2002)

13. Inputs from Vinod Rishi, Raman Sukumar and Vivek Menon

Chapter 11: A Yellow Taj Mahal

1. Bartholet, Jeffrey. 'How to Save the Taj Mahal?' Published in September, 2011. *Smithsonian* magazine

2. Likens, Gene E and Holmes Richard T. 'The Discovery of Acid Rain' Published on May 4, 2016. http://blog.yalebooks.com/2016/05/04/discovery-acid-rain/

3. 'Acid Rain'. United States Environmental Protection Agency. Accessed on January 4, 2020. https://www3.epa.gov/acidrain/education/site_students/caaa1990_back.html

4. Inputs from MC Mehta

Chapter 12: Uranium Poisoning in Punjab

1. Goswami, Subhojit. 'Uranium contamination in Punjab could be due to geological processes: study' Published on July 16, 2018. https://www.downtoearth.org.in/news/environment/uranium-contamination-in-punjab-could-be-due-to-geological-processes-study-61134

2. 'Groundwater contaminated, Punjab battles uranium curse'. Published on July 13, 2012. Indo Asian News Service.

3. 'Ground Water Quality Features of the Country' Accessed on February 15, 2020. Http://cgwb.gov.in/WQ/

GROUND%20WATER%20QUALITY%20SCENARIO%20
IN%20INDIA.pdf
4. Natural Resources Defense Council. 'The Story of Silent
Spring' Published on August 13, 2015 https://www.nrdc.
org/stories/story-silent-spring
5. Inputs from toxicologist Carin Smit

Chapter 13: India's 'Green' Court

1. 'Understanding the National Green Tribunal' Published
on July 27, 2016 https://www.cprindia.org/news/5400
2. 'Environmental Law and Policy: Environmental Activism'
Published on February 2, 2018. https://www.lawteacher.
net/free-law-essays/environmental-law/environmental-
law-and-policy-activism-law-essays.php
3. Chaudhari, Saumya. '2010-2020: Breaking Down the
National Green Tribunal Story' *Environmental Law
Quarterly: Paryavidi* Vol. I Issue 4 (October-December
2019)
4. Inputs from MC Mehta and Sanjay Upadhyay

Chapter 14: Mountains of Waste

1. Bisen, Ankur. *Wasted*. New Delhi: Pan Macmillan, 2019
2. Edited by Zimring Carl A. and Rathje William L.
*Encyclopedia of Consumption and Waste: The Social Science
of Garbage*. Sage Publications, 2012
3. Ramesh, Mridula. *The Climate Solution: India's Climate
Change Crisis and What We Can Do About It*. Gurgaon:
Hachette Book Publishing India Pvt Ltd, 2018
4. Subramanian, Nithya. 'Plastics: How a material that was
supposed to revolutionise the future became a dreaded

pollutant' Published on October 1, 2019. https://scroll.in/article/938452/plastics-how-a-material-that-was-supposed-to-revolutionise-the-future-became-a-dreaded-pollutant

5. Research unit (Larrdis) Rajya Sabha secretariat. "E-Waste in India' Published in June, 2011. https://rajyasabha.nic.in/rsnew/publication_electronic/E-Waste_in_india.pdf

6. Varkey 'The Global Waste Trade' Published on May 13, 2019 https://peoplesdispatch.org/2019/05/13/the-global-waste-trade/

7. Anand Y.P. 'Cleanliness-Sanitation: Gandhian Movement and Swachh Bharat Abhiyan' Accessed on April 4, 2020 https://www.mkgandhi.org/articles/cleanliness-sanitation-gandhian-movement-swachh-bharat-abhiyan.html

Chapter 15: Not a Drop to Drink

1. Ramesh, Mridula. *The Climate Solution: India's Climate Change Crisis and What We Can Do About It*. Gurgaon: Hachette Book Publishing India Pvt Ltd, 2018

2. Ramesh, Mridula. 'Chennai water crisis: Citizens' Day Zero experiences impacted by locality, income and consumption' Published on July 3, 2019 https://www.firstpost.com/india/chennai-water-crisis-citizens-experience-of-day-zero-impacted-by-locality-income-and-consumption-6914281.html

3. Vachcharajani, Bijal. *So You Want to Know About the Environment*. New Delhi: Rupa Publications India Pvt Ltd. 2017

4. 'What Makes up Freshwater?' Accessed on November 3, 2019. http://www.eschooltoday.com/global-water-scarcity/fresh-water-and-children.html

5. Shepherd, Marshall. 'Why Chennai Is Running Out of Water In 2 Satellite Images And An Explanation' Published on July 1, 2019. *Forbes*

6. https://chennaimetrowater.tn.gov.in/whatwhy.html

7. Mahesh Kumar S.T. 'With three rivers and five wetlands, why is Chennai staring at ecological collapse?' Published on February 6, 2017 https://chennai.citizenmatters. in/chennai-rivers-wetlands-marsh-environment-heritage-1577

8. Narayanan, Vivek. 'North Chennai: a bustling locality that's a heritage trove' Published on August 26, 2018. *The Hindu*

9. "Water crisis: 'rain effect' shots avoided in Kollywood" Published on June 30, 2019. *Deccan Herald*

10. Pandit, Atharva. 'Chennai water crisis: Here's all you need to know about it' Published on June 28, 2019 https:// www.moneycontrol.com/news/trends/current-affairs-trends/chennai-water-crisis-heres-all-you-need-to-know-about-it-4144491.html

11. Guntoju Sujith Sourab, Mohammad Faiz Alam, Sikka Alok. 'Chennai water crisis: A wake-up call for Indian cities' Published on August 5, 2019. https://www.downtoearth. org.in/blog/water/chennai-water-crisis-a-wake-up-call-for-indian-cities-66024

12. Bisen, Ankur. *Wasted*. New Delhi: Pan Macmillan, 2019

13. 'Composite Water Management Index: A Tool for Water Management' Published in June 2018 https://niti.gov.in/ writereaddata/files/document_publication/2018-05-18-Water-index-Report_vS6B.pdf

14. 'Traditional Water Harvesting Systems of India' Accessed on November 15, 2019 http://www.cpreec.org/pubbook-traditional.htm

15. Garcia, Meryl 'India's Water Warrior Has a Solution for India's Droughts. The Best Part – We Can Play a Role Too!' Published on March 5, 2016. https://www.thebetterindia.com/48298/ayyappa-masagi-water-warrior-conservation-rainwater-harvesting-water-gandhi-water-literacy-foundation/

16. 'Rani-ki-Vav (the Queen's Stepwell) at Patan, Gujarat' Accessed on November 15, 2019 https://whc.unesco.org/en/list/922

17. Wheeling, Kate. 'Major cities in India are starting to run out of water' Published on July 18, 2019. *The Week*

18. Ghoshal, Devjyot. 'Why does Chennai keep going under water?' Published November 19, 2015 https://scroll.in/article/770204/why-does-chennai-keep-going-under-water

19. Gopalakrishnan, Seetha. 'Muck tale: How Cooum lost its holy status' Published on April 20, 2017. https://www.indiawaterportal.org/articles/muck-tale-how-cooum-lost-its-holy-status

20. 'A short history of desalination' Published on June 3, 2015 http://www.theenergyofchange.com/short-history-of-desalination

21. 'Minjur Desalination Plant, Tamil Nadu, India' Accessed on November 15, 2019 https://www.water-technology.net/projects/minjurdesalination/

22. Ruiz, Irene Banos. 'Environmental cost of quenching world's thirst' Published on January 21, 2019 https://www.dw.com/en/

23. Ray, Isha and Prasad, CS Sharada. 'When the sewers get blocked: sanitation labour in urban India' Published on November 15, 2019. https://www.indiawaterportal.org/articles/when-sewers-get-blocked-sanitation-labour-urban-india

24. Vachcharajani, Bijal. *So You Want to Know About the Environment*. New Delhi: Rupa Publications India Pvt Ltd. 2017
25. James, Zhayynn. 'The guardians of the Seven Wells' Published in September, 2010 http://madrasmusings. com/Vol%2020%20No%2011/the_guardians_of_the_ seven_wells.html

Chapter 16: Smokin' Delhi

1. Narain, Sunita. *Conflicts of Interest: My Journey through India's Green Movement* Gurgaon: Penguin Random House India, 2017
2. 'Air Pollution in Delhi: An Analysis' Published in 2016 by the Envis Centre, Central Pollution Control Board
3. 'Explained: Bharat Stage IV emission norms and the history behind it' Published March 29, 2017, Business Standard
4. Kalavalapalli Yogendra, Raj Amrit and Shah Gouri. 'How Maruti 800 changed the dynamics of Indian car industry' Published on February 13, 2014 https://www. livemint.com/Companies/js6mNCIQXBVo5tnBnspzVI/ How-Maruti-800-changed-the-dynamics-of-Indian-car-industry.html
5. 'Review of Road Network and Transport System' Accessed on November 20, 2019 https://ccs.in/sites/default/files/ files/Ch11_Review%20of%20Road%20Network%20 and%20Transport%20System.pdf
6. Sivaramakrishnan, K and Rademacher, Anne. *Ecologies of Urbanism in India: Metropolitan Civility and Sustainability*. Hong Kong: Hong Kong University Press, 2013

7. Halder, Ritam 'By March 15, all industrial units in Delhi will switch to PNG: Govt tells EPCA' Published on January 4, 2018. *Hindustan Times*

8. Aggarwal, Mayank. 'Laws Meant to Save Water Unexpectedly Led to More Air Pollution: Study' Published on September 2, 2019 https://thewire.in/environment/laws-meant-to-save-water-unexpectedly-led-to-more-air-pollution-study

9. All information on Delhi Metro from http://www.delhimetrorail.com

10. Chakravartty, Anupam. 'Why three toddlers were forced to seek SC ban on firecrackers' Published on September 30, 2015. *Down To Earth*

Chapter 17: Powering the Future

1. 'Growth of electricity sector in India from 1947-2019' Report published in May 2019 by the Ministry of Power and Central Electricity Authority http://www.cea.nic.in/reports/others/planning/pdm/growth_2019.pdf

2. 'Eco India: A retired Botany professor in the city of Pune has never used electricity in her life' Published on March 3, 2019 https://scroll.in/video/914986/eco-india-a-retired-botany-professor-in-the-city-of-pune-has-never-used-electricity-in-her-life

3. 'What is renewable energy?' Accessed on December 2, 2019 https://www.alliantenergykids.com/RenewableEnergy/RenewableEnergyHome

4. Vasudevan Reshmi, Cherail Koshy, Bhatia Ramesh and Jayaram Nisha. *Energy Efficiency in India: History and Overview* New Delhi: Alliance for an Energy Efficient Economy, 2011

5. Bhattacharya S.C. and Jana Chinmoy. 'Renewable energy in India: Historical developments and prospects' Published on October 1, 2008 *Elsevier, Energy 34* (2009)
6. Ramesh, Mridula. *The Climate Solution: India's Climate Change Crisis and What We Can Do About It.* Gurgaon: Hachette Book Publishing India Pvt Ltd, 2018
7. Gopalakrishnan, Mukuteswara. 'Hydro Energy Sector in India: The Past, Present and Future Challenges' *Proceedings of the Indian National Science Academy* Vol 81 (2015)
8. Kharbanda V. P. and Qureshi M. A. 'Biogas Development in India and the PRC' *The Energy Journal* Vol 6, No. 3 (July 1985)
9. Sangroya Deepak and Nayak Jogendra Kumar. 'Development of Wind Energy in India' *International Journal of Renewable Energy Research* Vol 5, No. 1 (2015)
10. Kapoor Karan, Pandey Krishan K., Jain A.K. and Nandan Ashish. 'Evolution of solar energy in India: A review' *Elsevier Renewable and Sustainable Energy Reviews 40* (2014)
11. 'Where is Solar Power Used the Most?' Accessed on December 2, 2019 https://energyinformative.org/where-is-solar-power-used-the-most/
12. 'Green Building' Accessed on December 2, 2019 https://www.naturalstoneinstitute.org/default/assets/File/consumers/historystoneingreenbuilding.pdf
13. Nirman Consultants 'CII-Sohrabji Godrej Green Business Center, Hyderabad: A guiding light' Published on August 31, 2016 http://nirman.com/blog/2016/08/31/cii-sohrabji-godrej-green-business-center-hyderabad-a-guiding-light/
14. D'Cunha, Suparna Dutt 'Modi Announces "100% Village Electrification", But 31 Million Indian Homes Are Still In The Dark' Published on May 7, 2018, *Forbes*

15. Rath, Anubhav 'Indian Blackouts of July 2012: What Happened and Why?' Published on December 1, 2016 https://medium.com/clean-energy-for-billions/indian-blackouts-of-july-2012-what-happened-and-why-639e31fb52ad

Chapter 18: Waste in Space

1. Hall, Loretta 'The History of Space Debris' Published on November 6, 2014 https://commons.erau.edu/cgi/viewcontent.cgi?article=1000&context=stm
2. Davey, Melissa 'We've left junk everywhere: why space pollution could be humanity's next big problem' Published March 25, 2017 *The Guardian*
3. O'Callaghan, Jonathan 'What is space junk and why is it a problem?' Published on November 14, 2019 https://www.nhm.ac.uk/discover/what-is-space-junk-and-why-is-it-a-problem.html
4. Aerospace, 'Danger: Orbital Debris' Published on May 4, 2018 https://aerospace.org/article/danger-orbital-debris
5. Weeden, Brian. '2009 Iridium: Cosmos Collision Fact Sheet' Published on November 10, 2010 https://swfound.org/media/205392/swf_iridium_cosmos_collision_fact_sheet_updated_2012.pdf
6. National Research Council. *Orbital Debris: A Technical Assessment*. Washington, DC: The National Academies Press, 1995
7. Brito, T.P. et al, Journal of Physics: Conference Series 465 (2013)
8. Jeevan, S.S. 'Space Race 2.0: Orbits of debris' Published on May 12, 2019 https://www.downtoearth.org.in/blog/science-technology/space-race-2-0-orbits-of-debris-64265

9. Griffin, Andrew. 'Why Has India Shot Down a Satellite in Space and what is Mission Shakti?' Published on March 27, 2019 *Independent*

10. 'ISRO's Timeline from 1960s to Today' accessed on December 12, 2019 https://www.isro.gov.in/about-isro/isros-timeline-1960s-to-today#13

11. '50 Years of ISRO: Hits and misses in India's space journey' Published on August 16, 2019 *Business Today*

12. Ayyar, Kamakshi. 'How A Little Church In Kerala Helped India Reach For The Stars' Published on October 6, 2015 *National Geographic Traveller India*

12. Gannon, Megan 'The Scoop on Space Poop: How Astronauts Go Potty' Published on August 29, 2013. https://www.space.com/22597-space-poop-astronaut-toilet-explained.html

13. Billings, Lee 'Space Archaeologist Probes History in Orbit' Published on September 25, 2019 https://www.scientificamerican.com/article/space-archaeologist-probes-history-in-orbit/

Chapter 19: Climate Catastrophe

1. Ramesh, Mridula. *The Climate Solution: India's Climate Change Crisis and What We Can Do About It*. Gurgaon: Hachette Book Publishing India Pvt Ltd, 2018

2. Vachcharajani, Bijal. *So You Want to Know About the Environment*. New Delhi: Rupa Publications India Pvt Ltd. 2017

3. Dinwiddie Robert, Lamb Simon and Reynolds Ross. *Violent Earth*. London: Dorling Kindersley, 2011

4. *Climate Educator Guide* published on August 27, 2014 on https://www.rainforest-alliance.org/curricula/climate

5. Revkin, Andrew. 'Climate Change First Became News 30 Years Ago. Why Haven't We Fixed It?' Published in July 2018 *National Geographic*

6. Greshko, Michael and the National Geographic Staff. 'What are mass extinctions, and what causes them?' Published on September 26, 2019 https://www.nationalgeographic.com/science/prehistoric-world/mass-extinction/

7. Ross Robert S., Krishnamurti T. N., Pattnaik Sandeep & Pai D. S. *Decadal surface temperature trends in India based on a new high-resolution data set* Published on May 10, 2018 http://www.indiaenvironmentportal.org.in/files/file/surface%20temperature%20trends%20India.pdf

8. Banerji, Annie. 'It's official: India just experienced its hottest decade on record' Published on January 7, 2020 https://www.reuters.com/article/us-india-weather-temperature-trfn/its-official-india-just-experienced-its-hottest-decade-on-record-idUSKBN1Z61HK

9. 'India heatwave temperatures pass 50 Celsius' Published on June 2, 2019 on https://phys.org/news/2019-06-india-heatwave-temperatures-celsius.html

10. *Forest and Climate Change India: First Biennial Update Report to the United Nations Framework Convention on Climate Change* Published in December 2015 Ministry of Environment, Forest and Climate Change, Government of India

11. Dora Manoj & Kumar Padhee Arabinda. 'Cyclone Fani: Odisha teaches the world how to prepare for disasters' Published on May 15, 2019 *Business Standard*

12. Question on Rising Sea Level asked in Parliament, answered by Ashwini Kumar Choubey, Minister of State, Ministry of Health and Family Welfare https://moes.gov.in/writereaddata/files/LS_US_1119_28062019.pdf

13. Edited by Wester Philippus, Mishra Arabinda, Mukherji Aditi and Shrestha Arun Bhakta. *The Hindu Kush Himalaya Assessment: Mountains, Climate Change, Sustainability, People* Switzerland: Springer Nature, 2019
14. Edited by Lennard, Jeremy *Disaster Displacement: A Global Review, 2008-2019* Internal Displacement Monitoring Centre
15. Kumar Rohitashw and Gautam Harender Raj. 'Climate Change and its Impact on Agricultural Productivity in India' *Journal of Climatology & Weather Forecasting* Vol 2, Issue 1 (2014)
16. 'Climate change and health' Published on February 1, 2018 https://www.who.int/news-room/fact-sheets/detail/climate-change-and-health
17. Edited by Grillo, Oscar *Biodiversity: The Dynamic Balance of the Planet* Croatia: InTech, 2014
18. Behera, M.D., Behera, S.K. and Sharma, S. 'Recent advances in biodiversity and climate change studies in India'. *Biodiversity and Conservation* 28 (2019). https://doi.org/10.1007/s10531-019-01781-0

Chapter 20: National Action Plan for Climate Change

1. Ramesh, Mridula. *The Climate Solution: India's Climate Change Crisis and What We Can Do About It.* Gurgaon: Hachette Book Publishing India Pvt Ltd, 2018
2. Eckstein David, Künzel Vera, Schäfer Laura, Winges Maik. *Global Climate Risk Index 2020: Who suffers most from extreme weather events? Weather-related loss events in 2018 and 1999 to 2018* Bonn: Germanwatch, 2019 https://germanwatch.org/sites/germanwatch.org/files/20-

2-01e%20Global%20Climate%20Risk%20Index%20
2020_14.pdf

3. Pandve HT. 'India's National Action Plan on Climate Change'. *Indian Journal of Occupational and Environmental Medicine* 13(1) (2009) https://www.ncbi.nlm.nih.gov/pmc/articles/PMC2822162/

4. Rattani Vijeta, Venkatesh Shreeshan, Pandey Kundan, Jitendra, Kukreti Ishan, Somvanshi Avikal, Sangomla Akshit. 'India's National Action Plan on Climate Change needs desperate repair' Published on October 18, 2018 https://www.downtoearth.org.in/news/climate-change/india-s-national-action-plan-on-climate-change-needs-desperate-repair-61884

5. Country Summary: India. Accessed on December 16, 2019 https://climateactiontracker.org/countries/india/

6. Inputs from N. Ravindranath